silience

"This book successfully integrates the lessons learned from thousands of years of Eastern meditation tradition with the latest findings of Western science. For novices and experts alike, it will broaden and deepen your understanding. I have meditated in the peace and quiet of a mountain retreat and as a combat soldier in trenches. Meditation is a powerful tool to develop focus, peace, and clarity. This is the best book on meditation I have ever read."

— John Gibbons, practicing psychologist for forty years

"At a time when work life is getting faster and more complex, we all need to clear our minds and develop focus. It is an absolute must for high-performance work environments. This book makes building mental re-silience easy. It has helped me as a mother, a partner, and an executive."

— Elizabeth Broderick, partner, Blake Dawson Waldron

"This book gets to the crux of how to clear your mind and develop men-tal focus. This technique has been an inspiration for many executives in developing their mental resilience and levels of peace to reduce stress and function at their peak."

— Les Fallick, CEO, Principle Advisory Services

"It is said that our lives are determined not by the things that happen to us but by how we react to them. This is true both professionally and personally. Being able to focus clearly, by clearing our increasingly cluttered mind, is a prerequisite for success. Kamal teaches easy-to-use and practical techniques to obtain mental resilience. I have found his teachings incredibly useful in just about all aspects of my life."

— Rob Prugue, managing director,
Lazard Asset Management, Asia Pacific division

"Athletes are taught not only how to train but also to rest their physical bodies so that they can recuperate after periods of intense competition.

In corporate life we continually make intense mental demands of our staff without always taking the appropriate measures to truly assist them in resting their minds. The Mental Resilience Training techniques described in this book allow us all to maintain peak mental performance so that we can thrive rather than get bogged down with the stresses of modern work life."

— Colin Pitt, general manager for Learning and Performance,
St. George Bank

"Developing mental flexibility is extremely important in corporate life. This book is full of insights into a most-perplexing contemporary dilemma: how to keep your most precious asset, your mind, in its naturally resilient state."

— Kate Mulligan, managing director, Advance Funds Management

"Truly fulfilled people must have mental resilience. Leaders at any level must have clarity and focus. The technique and skills taught in this book and audio have transformed my life. These techniques are relevant for any part of your life, in the bedroom or the boardroom."

— Dan Dumitrescu, global head of technology,
Edward W. Kelly & Partners

"For those of us with busy lives, our greatest regret may be that of failing to seize the moment and truly be present to the reality of our lives as it unfolds. Constantly being somewhere else mentally is one of the major causes of stress and exhaustion. The tools in this book can help all people be truly present to their lives so they can thrive rather than just exist."

— Bettina Pidcock, director of marketing, Asgard Wealth Solutions

mental resilience

mental resilience

the power of clarity

how to develop
the focus of a warrior
and the peace of a monk

Kamal Sarma

New World Library
Novato, California

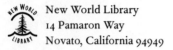 New World Library
14 Pamaron Way
Novato, California 94949

Text design by Tona Pearce Myers
Author photograph by David Starr

"Eating Mindfully" exercise on page 166 used with permission from www.MindfulEating.org, copyright © 2004 by DayOne Publishing. All rights reserved.

Library of Congress Cataloging-in-Publication Data
Sarma, Kamal, 1967–
Mental resilience : the power of clarity : how to develop the focus of a warrior and the peace of a monk / Kamal Sarma.
    p. cm.
Includes bibliographical references and index.
ISBN 978-1-57731-625-1 (pbk. : alk. paper)
1. Meditation. I. Title.
BL627.S372 2008
158.1'2—dc22   2007050765

First printing, March 2008
ISBN: 978-1-57731-625-1
Printed in Canada on 100% postconsumer-waste recycled paper

New World Library is a proud member of the Green Press Initiative.

10 9 8 7 6 5 4

To all the warrior monks who stand up against oppression and violence with only their focus, peace, and compassion. To those who fight not with arms but with alms.

contents

from monastery to management

*We will only understand the miracle of life fully
when we allow the unexpected to happen.*

PAULO COELHO

THE INITIAL IDEA TO WRITE THIS BOOK began with a trip to my local bookstore. I was looking for a book on meditation, not just any kind of book or any kind of meditation. I did find a lot of books on meditation but none that fit the bill. There were books by enlightened sages or saints of some religious persuasion. Those by New Age authors featured pages packed with soft-focus photos and lists of affirmations that promised a personal nirvana. Those written by philosophers and academics had lengthy eulogies on the theoretical aspects of meditation but failed to address the very practical steps people would need to take if they asked, "So how do I start meditating? What do I do next? How will it affect my life? How do I know I am doing it right? How will this make me mentally resilient?"

I have practiced meditation for the past twenty years and have taught it for the past eight. Since recently starting to teach it in corporations, I realized that a book could provide a tool kit, a practical guide for my students' ongoing reference and practice.

With this book, I hope to fill a gap that I found when looking for a plainspoken guide. My approach to teaching meditation is to provide information free of jargon or hype. This book will give you the tools to begin a meditation practice and, through it, develop a more resilient and clear mind. I call this technique Mental Resilience Training.

How to Use This Book

This book contains two parts: "Theory" (see part 1, chapters 1 through 4) and "Practice" (see part 2, chapters 5 through 12). If you are eager to get started, start with "Practice" and return to "Theory" when you're ready.

To help you get started, an audio download with Mental Resilience Training exercises accompanies this book. (Go to www.mentalresilience.com to download the files. The exercises are at various levels and are designed for different purposes. You can use the audio in conjunction with the explanations in the book or on its own. If you have always wanted to try meditation but weren't sure how, simply find a comfortable place to be, put the audio on, listen, and away you'll go.

You can start using these techniques immediately. I have deliberately kept the theory light, but it shows how the process of meditation works, what signposts you may encounter, and what others have experienced along this amazing internal journey.

The audio is also a resource you can return to whenever you need some support in your practice. When you use it with the book, you have the complete tool kit to help you learn to meditate.

Why I Wrote This Book

First, let me confess that I am not a saintly man. I am an ordinary workingman, making my way in the mesh of activities and relationships that comprise a management role in a commercial environment. Yet I have found the practice of meditation to be my most valuable skill. In fact, I believe meditation is more relevant for managers, mothers, and entrepreneurs — ordinary people — than it is for monks and nuns. Meditation is more pertinent for people living in the world, who are not sitting high in the mountains trying to figure out the meaning of life. As I wrote this book, my wife and I had to deal with a brain-tumor scare, two babies in intensive care, the breakup of a business, and living with a chronic illness.

Mental Resilience Training:
My Approach to Meditation

My meditation practice has helped me through both personal and professional crises. Let me explain why I approach meditation the way I do.

I was born in Assam, in northeastern India, near the border between Tibet and Burma. Because my family moved to Australia when I was five years old, I was desperate to be a normal Australian young boy. Life was full of meat pies, Vegemite, sports, movies, and girls — the usual stuff.

When I was thirteen, my father accepted work as a missionary doctor in Karnataka, so the family moved back to India. My parents were very protective of me and, fearing I would give in to peer pressure (illicit drug taking, in particular), sent me to a monastery (ashram) to continue my education. Instead of living the normal life of a suburban Australian teenager — going to a coed school, enjoying family holidays at the beach, driving around in a big car — I found myself in a very different world. Life in the monastery meant sleeping on a concrete floor, getting up at 4:30 AM, taking cold showers, giving up eating meat, and following a life of poverty. To say this was a culture shock would be an understatement.

While at the monastery, I learned to read and write Sanskrit and studied major religious texts — the Bible, including the Torah; Bhagavad Gita; and Koran. Although it was predominantly a Hindu ashram, we were encouraged to study all the major texts so that we could see how similar most religious approaches were. This discipline and study were all too much for me. As a thirteen-year-old, I really just wanted to read comics, not the Vedas (ancient Indian sacred texts). Frustrated with the rules and regulations that were part of monastery life, I sometimes sneaked out and vented my teenage angst by taking long treks in the nearby hills. On one of these expeditions, I met Nanda, an ascetic who lived alone in a small, simple hut near the monastery. It was Nanda who introduced me to meditation and influenced my eventual development of Mental Resilience Training.

Nanda had studied yoga and meditation for many years. This gave him a supple body and calm approach to life, and though I never knew his age, I'm certain he was far older than he looked. Although I was bucking against the authority of the monastery, I found myself fascinated by Nanda. When he offered to teach me a deeper level of yoga and meditation, I jumped at the chance. I always struggle when I try to describe Nanda, because he is so hard to summarize. More than anything, Nanda was at peace with himself and his surroundings.

I figured Nanda was about eighty-five years old, but he looked about fifty. His skin was taut, with a beautiful glow, and his face had a gentle, feminine quality. The whites of his eyes were very white and clear, with a piercing quality. He did not look strong and was instead a bit scrawny, but he could hold a handstand for over ten minutes on a cliff's edge. Most people would consider him handsome in a grandfatherly way. But perhaps the most intriguing and, for me, important aspect of Nanda was that he had more faith in me than I had in myself.

Nanda was a very erudite man. He could quote Shakespeare and Socrates, and relate their ideas back to the mind and how it works. He had been trained in physics and mathematics, and thus used many scientific analogies in my training. Nanda taught me how to be aware of the power of my emotions, how not to be overwhelmed by the extremes I sometimes felt. During my lessons, he often said that there was no textbook for my mind, that I had to find my own way.

"A teacher can only show the way," he said, "but you have to climb the mountain yourself. So, the less emotional baggage you take up with you, the easier it is." Nanda told me to be wary of people who claimed to be more spiritual than me, who might claim that they could "take me up the mountain" on their backs. He was a tough taskmaster, who did not allow me to be lazy with my practice.

These early lessons provided me with the keys I had craved so that I could discover the full potential of my mind. I learned to stretch both my body and mind in ways I had not even imagined possible. A lot of teenagers spend time in the gym pumping iron and taking care of their developing bodies. I took this approach to my mind. As Nanda said, "You have a beautiful, resilient, and radiant mind; you just need to take care of it."

I stayed in the ashram for five years, running off to see Nanda almost every day. I sometimes practiced with him for over twelve hours a day, spending very little time on my academic studies. However, due to his training, I found that I could perform well without spending much time with my books. Since my mind was so clear and focused, I could study for only a little while, confident that I could recall the knowledge at will.

Although I regarded Nanda as very special, I did not realize how lucky or blessed I was to train with him. As a teenager I did not recognize the true value of what he was teaching me. Only later did I realize that Nanda had planted seeds in my mind that "only would fertilize with the manure of life" (his words). I never forgot Australia, and I missed it dearly. I always felt that Australia was home, so I hankered to return there.

At the age of nineteen, I returned to Australia and went to a university. I studied economics and earned an MBA. Drawn to the promises of corporate life, I followed the herd after graduation. My first serious job was with one of the world's leading management-consulting firms, McKinsey and Company. McKinsey provides advice to organizations around the world, and in my role, I presented strategies for multimillion-dollar projects to very influential people in powerful companies, advising them on how to increase profitability. I flew business class across the world, staying at five-star hotels and paying for it all with my corporate expense account. I had come a long way from living a life of humility and poverty in a monastery.

As with many similar professional organizations, McKinsey's corporate culture was one of "work hard, play hard." Many workdays began at 7:30 AM and finished at 11:00 PM. I had desperately wanted to be successful, and while at McKinsey, I thought I was. I lived the corporate jet-setter life, centered on the next flight, the next deadline, and the next hotel room. But during this time I also forgot the benefits of being still, both in body and mind.

I have discovered that all human evil comes from this:
man's being unable to sit still and quiet in a room alone.

BLAISE PASCAL

McKinsey was a great training ground, because my life was focused on adding value for the shareholders and putting clients' needs before my own. I was engrossed by it all. I was also amazed by the inordinate amount of power that such large, globally active corporations had. It excited me but frightened me too. In some situations, our work had the potential to drastically change the economy of communities, or even nations, and could impact future generations. What also frightened me was the mental state that some of these executives were in while making these huge decisions. I remember a CEO who was going through a messy divorce. He felt very bitter and twisted by the whole saga, and mentioned that he had trouble sleeping, could not think straight, and felt depressed. He would come into the office dressed in an Armani suit and cuff links, appearing supremely confident, but every now and then he admitted that he felt as if he were falling apart at the seams. On top of all this, he was asked to make decisions that would likely change the lives of thousands of people and the environment for many years to come.

One of the most important lessons I learned during my time with McKinsey was a new way to approach problems, a technique that underpins my business career to this day. I learned that effective decision making requires a hypothesis. The path that leads to a particular decision is guided by research and analysis to support or disprove the hypothesis. At that point, my life was completely based on analysis and logic. My younger life was based on faith, which had allowed me to just *believe* something was true, but this was no longer valid. Now, I was deeply immersed in a world where facts, logic, and reason were the ultimate evidence.

Some years after leaving McKinsey, I married my university sweetheart, a doctor who practices medicine in Sydney. We bought a house and settled down. I was living the suburban dream and busily climbing the corporate ladder. Life was fantastic.

But when I was about thirty, my life hit a massive brick wall.

My wife was pregnant with our first child, and we were as excited as any young couple could be. She is very devoted to her medical practice in one of the more socially and economically challenged parts of Sydney. On a routine check seven weeks before our baby was due, her obstetrician admitted her to the hospital for bed rest; because my wife is a dedicated doctor, bed rest would guarantee the rest she needed. On her second night in the hospital, I got a call in the middle of the night that indicated she was delivering. During the thirty long minutes it took me to get to her, my wife had to undergo an emergency Cesarean section.

On reaching the hospital, I was told that I was extremely lucky: my wife had suffered complications, but the surgical team had managed to save her life. They also told me I was the father of a baby girl, but due to complications she was in intensive care. My heart racing with excitement and hands clammy with stress, I simultaneously felt joy and dread.

At 3:00 AM, the doctors told us that our daughter was in bad shape and they would need to monitor her closely. But by late morning she was much better. Things looked positive and we all felt relieved. I remember touching my child for the first time and realizing how incredible it felt. I also remember the pain of seeing her tiny body with tubes and needles inserted into her soft skin.

After three days in the hospital, her condition deteriorated so severely that we had to make the painful decision to remove her life support. That night was the most devastating night in my life. The sounds and smells of that night are chiseled into my psyche. Such moments define your life, and everything you thought was important falls away.

I can still remember the piercing beep of the monitor that tracked the fluids being pumped into her tiny body; the lightness, almost nothingness, of the weight of her body; the pinkness of her beautifully formed lips; the sharp smell of the hospital antiseptic;

and the cries of healthy babies in the ward who wanted to be nursed by their mothers. The total despair of that night was unforgettable. Looking down at her, I realized that a wonderful being who had been a gift was now being taken away from us, and there was absolutely nothing I could do about it except cry. As the sun rose, our beautiful baby daughter died silently in my arms. Suddenly my life had become horrific.

My wife and I struggled to maintain both our sanity and our marriage. The grief and guilt were overwhelming. When we came back from the hospital, the grief started to mix with depression, and my life began to nose-dive. I wanted to stay in bed and curl into a ball and cry. When the crying stopped, I felt numb. I struggled to get up and go to work. When I eventually got there, I was incapable of doing much. At that time I worked in investment management with Australia's largest fund manager. I had to deal with senior executives from top organizations daily. I needed to make significant decisions. I needed to perform 100 percent of the time. Being unproductive for a few hours was bad, but being paralyzed with grief and guilt for a whole day was a disaster. I was in real fear of losing my job. My mind felt dull and sluggish, causing me to slip into a continual state of mental blur. The heaviness in my chest just would not go away, and the void in my stomach just kept getting deeper.

Nothing I did could relieve the helplessness I felt. I tried alcohol, but it just made me feel sick. I contemplated drugs and psychiatric medication but knew that they just masked symptoms and would leave me feeling even hollower. My body seemed to be falling apart; I lost around thirty pounds in less than two weeks. I wanted the overwhelming feeling of depression to go away, but nothing would get rid of it. I thought of suicide on a number of occasions.

I felt as if I were trying to put my mind into gear, but all I could hear was the crunching of the gears. How could I get my mind to bounce back? How could let go of this pain? I did not want to numb my mind; I wanted to regain my clarity and focus. I wanted to regain my mind's ability to make decisions, to serve me so that I could serve people around me. I knew my mind had been resilient before; I knew that if I could somehow stop this incessant chatter, I could do the things that had been so easy before. But from my viewpoint at the time, I could not even begin to imagine that it would ever be possible.

During those dark days, one option that kept occurring to me was meditation. I wondered if I could use it to regain the mental resilience I realized I had lost. It had been years since I had practiced, as if a lifetime had passed since I had trekked out to Nanda's hut for my lessons, but somewhere deep in my mind, I had a sense that meditation might be the solution to my grief and depression.

Desperate for something to wrench me out of my despair, I read some meditation books to remind me of the techniques, but I found that they no longer had any resonance. The techniques seemed to be full of mumbo jumbo and relied on a foundation of faith. I needed something different now; I needed a tool to discipline my mind so that I could return to the everyday world with a new practice, one that was experiential and grounded in the practicality of ordinary life.

I read all that I could get my hands on and tried to strip all the information to its bare bones to uncover the fundamentals of the meditation being espoused. In dissecting the information I was gathering, I began to release the ritual cats that made meditation confusing (see the following box). What I ended up with was a simple practice that focused on developing mental resilience and clarity. I call this method Mental Resilience Training.

RITUAL CATS

Once upon a time, there was a teacher who had a pet cat. When he and his disciples sat down to meditate in the evening, the cat would make a lot of noise. This distracted the students terribly, because they did not have the same ability to concentrate as their master. To be kind to his students and assist in their practice, the teacher decided the cat should be tied up before the meditation practice. This went on for many years. When the teacher passed away, the cat continued to be tied up during the meditation sessions. Once the cat grew old and died, another cat was brought into the monastery and tied up. After many generations, the teacher's decendants wrote scholarly texts on the religious significance of cats and their importance to the meditation process.

My return to meditation ultimately lifted me out of my downward spiral. I still felt pain and grief over the loss of our daughter, but through my practice I was able to compartmentalize this grief so that it no longer paralyzed me. My mind regained its original power and focus, and I began to function again and enjoy my life.

I now practice meditation daily and teach it to my friends and colleagues, from successful entrepreneurs to stay-at-home mothers and fathers overseeing busy households. The members of this diverse group have several things in common: they engage in relationships, face conflicting demands, have little time, have to meet difficult deadlines, get sick, and feel angry or sad — just like me. The meditation practice I teach provides the skills to cope with these day-to-day pressures, fostering greater mental resilience.

When the mind is at peace, the world, too, is at peace.

J. KRISHNAMURTI

Frequently Asked Questions

Why Mental Resilience Training? Many people are put off by the word *meditation*, due to the religious or New Age connotations. However, these same people have no qualms about going to a gym when they feel physically weak. Meditation is about keeping the mind strong, clear, and resilient. I call this technique Mental Resilience Training because it helps keep the mind clear and strong without religious implications.

Can I learn to meditate without a teacher? When I learned to meditate, I was fortunate to have a private teacher. My teacher got to know my psychological makeup and then developed a meditation practice based on these traits and my personal hot spots. I was extremely lucky to have had such a personalized practice.

However, it is still possible to acquire a strong and effective meditation practice without personal instruction. The techniques described in this book and the exercises provided on the audio are suitable for anyone facing pressures and stress in work and personal life. They are suited to anyone who wants to learn how to delve into the mind; stop the seeming chaos and clutter; and find the right tools to increase clarity, resilience, and, ultimately, peacefulness and productivity. You can achieve a very effective practice by using the techniques in this book. However, if you want to pursue your meditation practice further, it can help to attend a weekend or week-long meditation retreat.

How long will it take me to learn how to meditate? Studies show that most people take twenty-one days to transform new behaviors into new habits. So, while I cannot promise mystical results or a magic potion that can heal all your ills, I can promise that if you commit to twenty-one days of practicing meditation (using this book and the audio with the suggested program in chapter 12), you will definitely realize these benefits: clarity of mind and mental resilience. It is written in the Vedas, "If you want to dig a well, it's no use digging a few meters and then stopping and trying somewhere else. You have to keep at it for a while." This adage applies to your journey with meditation. We live in an age where gratification is often instant. The latest news is online or on the television or radio. If we want to communicate with a friend or colleague overseas, we pick up the phone or send an email. When hungry, we grab fast food. As a result, we have become increasingly impatient. Meditation is not an instant thing; unlike with coffee, the buzz is unlikely to come immediately.

For meditation to have the required results for your well-being, you need to take the time to slow down and see what's really going on inside. Just as if you were rediscovering a long-lost friend, learning about yourself takes a while to happen.

I know meditators who have practiced for twenty years and still consider themselves beginners. Each time they sit for meditation, they find something new and wondrous about themselves that makes them even more resilient. However, even if you meditate for one minute or even one heartbeat, you will start receiving some of the benefits. Just as setting down a heavy bag for a moment gives you relief, so will a mere moment's meditation provide calm. It will also enable you to carry that heavy load even farther.

PART ONE

theory

If I had eight hours to chop down a tree,
I'd spend six hours sharpening my axe.

ABRAHAM LINCOLN

CHAPTER ONE

meditation — why bother?

*Everything is changing; let go a little at a time
and breathe new life into your old ways of thinking and feeling.
Let not fear be a complete barrier to the unknown.*

ANONYMOUS

MOST PEOPLE COME TO MEDITATION thinking, or even fearing, that it is difficult. No matter how much some people rave about the benefits of meditation, many think it would be easier to relax by merely playing a sport, reading a book, grabbing a drink, watching TV, or doing any number of things that don't require much effort.

Meditation does require some effort, or personal discipline, and it takes up the most precious commodity in our lives — time. Yet, to derive all of the benefits takes practice. So why go to all the trouble of learning to meditate? Isn't it all too hard? The short answer is that learning to meditate will invariably help your well-being. One of the best answers is that you will feel the benefits almost immediately, which is definitely one of the greatest aspects of meditation. I like to think of meditation as an insurance policy to protect your most precious asset — your mind.

The Benefits of Meditation

The core benefit of meditation is that it's a proven way to truly rest and clear your mind. We know how important it is to rest our body. We could not keep going for days on end without resting. We do not work most machines continuously without giving them a rest, for fear they might heat up and explode. But somehow, when it comes to resting our minds, we imagine the same laws don't apply.

Most people consider sleep to be the best way to rest and rejuvenate their minds. But a growing problem in today's world is that sleep does not equal rest for many people. And the lack of mental rest is not merely caused by lack of sleep, because when we sleep, we keep processing information from the day or other issues that needed but did not get our attention. In essence, we still use our minds during sleep. It is not easy to give the mind the real rest it craves.

We also have the notion that we can rest our minds when we go on vacation or just take time away from our normal life. How many times have you been on vacation, sitting on a lovely beach or walking in the green hills somewhere, when suddenly — *pop!* — up comes some worry or concern? How often has the stress of day-to-day life reemerged in your head the minute your relaxing vacation was over?

What is happening is that — despite attempts to relax, distract, and slow down — the mind still processes problems in your conscious and unconscious spheres. To truly stop the clutter and "traffic," we need to control our flow of thoughts and our brain waves. Meditation is a way to do just that. Through meditation we develop the skills and power to relax and clear our minds, and through this comes rest and a great many more benefits.

What would you say if I told you that by practicing meditation you could have the following benefits?

- Improved career performance and prospects
- Better health in body and mind
- Enhanced love life!

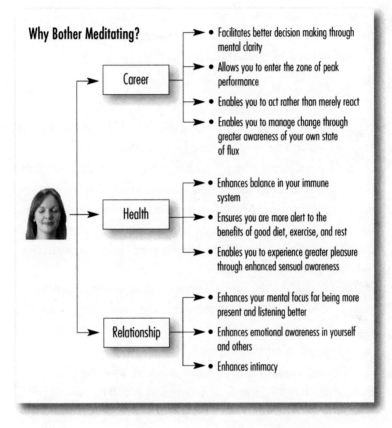

Why Bother Meditating?

Career
- Facilitates better decision making through mental clarity
- Allows you to enter the zone of peak performance
- Enables you to act rather than merely react
- Enables you to manage change through greater awareness of your own state of flux

Health
- Enhances balance in your immune system
- Ensures you are more alert to the benefits of good diet, exercise, and rest
- Enables you to experience greater pleasure through enhanced sensual awareness

Relationship
- Enhances your mental focus for being more present and listening better
- Enhances emotional awareness in yourself and others
- Enhances intimacy

I imagine that some of you might smile and thank me, while thinking, "Yeah, sure; how gullible do you think I am?" Well, it is true. For centuries warriors and monks alike have recognized the benefits of meditation. Today, contemporary health and medical professionals are confirming their assertions.

How Meditation Can Help Your Career

Many of us are paid to use our minds to add value to the organizations and communities we work in. To do this, we must have the clarity to make better decisions and the ability to focus our minds to the task at hand, so that we use more of our mental capacities. By actively training in these two areas, we can enhance our careers and offer more value.

Better Decision-Making Skills

It is in moments of decision making when we add or destroy value to ourselves and the people around us. The decisions may be large or small, but theoretically, for each of them, we gather as much information as we can, analyze that information, weigh our options, and make a decision. Some decisions may involve spending vast sums of money that carry huge consequences for the lives and livelihoods of many people. Other decisions might concern how to better serve a client's needs.

If you work in the medical profession or in law enforcement, your decisions sometimes involve life and death. And, astonishingly, these decisions often need to be made rapidly, sometimes in a matter of minutes or seconds.

The most important factor in effective and sound decision making is clarity of mind. If your mind is full of mental noise or distracting thoughts, then it will have to work harder, and take longer, to process information and make decisions. Additionally, if you have unconstructive emotions bubbling up inside you, your mind will likely feel fatigued, and your decisions won't necessarily be congruent with your internal values. Instead, your decisions will be based on the mental clutter whirring around in your mind.

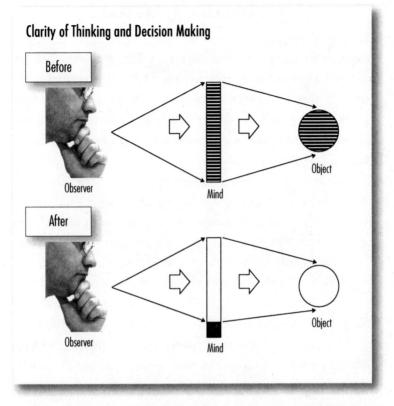

Clarity of Thinking and Decision Making

Before

Observer

Mind

Object

After

Observer

Mind

Object

In the "Before" phase of the illustration above, the thinker's mind is full of mental chatter. As a result, he can't clearly perceive the object at hand. By contrast, with Mental Resilience Training he is able to settle his mind and focus effectively on the object to make an insightful and effective decision.

Once you establish a sustained meditation practice, you become aware of the mental chatter and more adept at clearing it. You have the tools to develop some space to perceive a situation with greater clarity before you make any crucial decisions. The time you need to create this mental space is not hours or days; it is, literally, a few moments.

Enhanced Ability to Focus

Through the discipline of learning to focus on a single point, you will gain the skills to do your best work. Many athletes speak of entering a zone of peak performance where they are deeply attuned to whatever they need to do: hit or catch the ball, vault over a pole, or run a track. Meditation can help you harness mental energy so that you reach such a zone where you become focused. And you can do it with relative ease.

Similarly, if you have confidence in your ability to enter that zone of peak performance by bringing all of your mental energy to one precise point (for a customer, presentation, or report), you can be certain that you are using your maximum mental capacity. You will have hit that sweet spot of your own intellect.

A very important benefit of learning to focus is that, when you go home, even after a grueling workday, you will be able to compartmentalize and ensure that your mind is fully present and clear for your loved ones rather than remaining preoccupied with solving work issues. Other aspects of meditation's benefits will be covered in later chapters. Here, it is sufficient to say that meditation will enable you to gain the following skills:

- Act rather than react.
- Manage change through greater awareness of your own state of flux.

The Health Benefits of Meditation

Our minds are the biggest contributors to our physiological well-being. If we are mentally resilient we can manage our stress and truly give our bodies what they require, not through willpower, which can wax and wane, but through clarity, which gets stronger and stronger over time.

Stress Reduction

Stress is detrimental to our health. The *New England Journal of Medicine* states that "managing the long-term effects of the physiological responses to stress" is critical to survival.[1] Stress attacks nearly every major system in our bodies, creating myriad health problems including diabetes, high blood pressure, stroke, allergies, asthma, and colitis, to name a few; and is, reportedly, implicated in 85 percent of all medical problems. An indication of this simmering health crisis is the increase in the number of lawsuits brought against companies by employees affected by stress-related illnesses. Employers are now even more aware than in the past of their duty to provide stress-management techniques to employees who deal with stressful situations as part of their work.

Stress is not all bad. In fact, it is an important part of everyday functioning. It stimulates the body for action and, indirectly, has helped the human race survive. Our metabolism reacts to outside stimuli with a fight-or-flight response, and in this way, stress enables us to survive.[2]

When we feel stress, our body releases hormones like adrenaline. We may be reacting to physical or mental threats: if a boss criticizes us, for example, we may respond physiologically in exactly the same way that we did in prehistoric times when trying to escape the jaws of a particularly ravenous carnivore. Now, of course, hitting your boss on the head, which could be a strongly career-limiting move, or running like crazy, which could decrease your likelihood of getting paid, would not be appropriate reactions. But the released hormones do get our metabolism racing, and if the physical threat were real, such a response could save our lives.

So, it's important to know that not all stress is detrimental. But, like most things in life, you can overdo any good thing. And, most of the time, our response is inappropriate to the threat. If you are stressed for a long period because of work pressures, a demanding partner or children, and financial worries, your fight-or-flight responses start to attack your own body. The automatic mechanism built to defend your body now starts damaging it by blocking your arteries, knocking out your immune system, and overloading your endocrine system until, one day, you succumb to a cold if you are lucky or a serious illness if you're not.

Stress hormones act as painkillers. This analgesic effect explains stories we have heard of athletes who kept playing their games despite injury, unaware that they may have even broken bones or sustained other harm. Sometimes it isn't until hours later that they realize the extent of the damage and begin to experience the depth of the pain.

This happens in daily life as well. We work tirelessly throughout the day, ignoring our feelings. When feeling tired, we may pump ourselves up with that double shot of espresso. When we get headaches, we take painkillers. We take an antacid for an upset stomach. All the time, we ignore the signs of stress and simply treat its symptoms. But one day, the body may react violently with a serious illness such as heart attack, cancer, infection, or depression. If the immune system is out of balance, we suffer disease. So how can we avoid this?

Clinical studies have shown that meditation enables the immune system, our main defense against illness, to return to balance. The following table outlines some of the illnesses that result from an immune system that is out of balance. For example, if you have an inner stimulus such as emotional distress combined with an underactive immune system, you are particularly susceptible to getting cancer. You are more prone to suffer from autoimmune diseases (such as lupus or arthritis) if you have an overactive immune system.[3] (I am asserting not that meditation will prevent these ailments but rather that people who are less stressed and have balanced immune systems may have a better chance of staying well and resisting the onset of these diseases.)

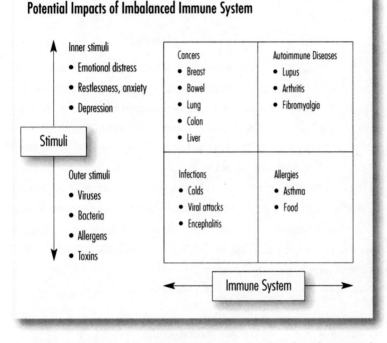

Potential Impacts of Imbalanced Immune System

Inner stimuli • Emotional distress • Restlessness, anxiety • Depression	Cancers • Breast • Bowel • Lung • Colon • Liver	Autoimmune Diseases • Lupus • Arthritis • Fibromyalgia
Outer stimuli • Viruses • Bacteria • Allergens • Toxins	Infections • Colds • Viral attacks • Encephalitis	Allergies • Asthma • Food

Stimuli

Immune System

Through Mental Resilience Training we develop the mental muscles to deeply rest the mind. We start clearing it of all the stressful thoughts that move through it, day in and day out. The rested mind allows the body to come back into harmony and the immune system to find a healthy balance.

Clinical Research Supporting Mental Resilience Training

There has been significant medical research on the benefits of the meditative aspects of Mental Resilience Training. While meditation practitioners have known the effects for centuries, only recently have scientific investigations given credence to these ancient claims. I have summarized some of this research here, but these findings are just the tip of the iceberg.

The Power of Attention

Indian researcher and professor B.K. Anand found that yogis could meditate themselves into trances so deep that they didn't react when hot test tubes were pressed against their arms. He also found that they could regulate their heartbeats at will.[4] In the book, *Zen Meditation and Psychotherapy*, Japanese scientist Tomio Hirai studied and measured the brain activity of forty Zen monks. He showed that longtime Zen meditators were so focused on the present moment that they had never habituated themselves to the sound of a ticking clock. Most people eventually become desensitized to such noises, but the meditators remained aware of it for hours on end. Instead of zoning out in their meditations, they were able to maintain a high level of awareness and focus.[5]

All We Need Is Love
(or a Bigger Left-Prefrontal Cortex)

In his work at the University of Wisconsin at Madison, Richard Davidson observed Buddhist monks' brain activity during their meditations, using the latest technologies, including functional magnetic resonance imaging (fMRI) and electroencephalograms (EEGs). Davidson found a much greater level of activity in the left prefrontal lobes of meditating monks' brains than of non-meditators. Further studies have shown that even after a short period of regular meditation, ordinary people can develop more activity in the left-prefrontal cortex. This area of the brain is said to be the home of peace and acceptance.[6]

Davidson has shown that through regular meditation the brain is reoriented from a stressful fight-or-flight mode to one of acceptance, a shift that increases contentment. This change is directly correlated with a shift in prefrontal activity. People with a negative disposition tend to be right-prefrontal oriented, whereas people with a left-prefrontal orientation are more enthusiastic, have more interests, take time to relax more, and tend to feel more content, without buying a Ferrari or a penthouse.

Davidson explains that the reason these people may feel happier has to do with neurotransmitters. Chemicals that carry signals from one neuron to another, neurotransmitters are your body's communication system. The prefrontal cortex is filled with various kinds of neurotransmitters, such as dopamine, glutamate, and serotonin. All these chemicals have been linked with positive emotional states. Certain studies with animals show that dopamine is very active in the signal transfer of positive emotions between the left-prefrontal area and the emotional center in the brain.

At Stanford University, Brian Knutson also conducted meditation research using fMRI. The result reported similar outcomes: participants who meditated had more left-prefrontal lobe activity than those who didn't meditate. This research confirms that meditation increases activity in the left side of the frontal region.[7] We know that when this area of the brain is more active, we have an increase in positive emotions and motivation. We are strengthened in our resolve to meet our goals.

Davidson also studied the effects of meditation on health. In this study, flu vaccines were given to two groups; one group received only the vaccine, while the other received the vaccine and were conducted in meditation. The results showed that the meditation group had a more significant increase in antibody levels than the control group. This confirms what many have said about meditation's effects of increased health and immunity.

How Having a Thicker Head Eases Aging

One of the benefits of Mental Resilience Training is equanimity, the feeling that we have the energy to adapt and handle life's trials. Research has shown that our brains actually become more robust after undertaking this type of training.

Neuroreport published research undertaken by Sara Lazar and her team at Harvard indicating that the areas of the brain linked with attention, interoception, and sensory processing (including the prefrontal cortex and right-anterior insular cortex) were thicker in participants who meditated than in control participants. There were distinct differences in the prefrontal cortical thickness of older participants between the two groups, directly associated with meditation, which indicates that meditation might delay the cortical thinning that occurs in the aging process. This research offered the first scientific evidence of cortical elasticity linked to meditation practice.[8] This basically means that your brain becomes tougher or more resilient, which can help counter the effects of aging as you grow older. This is a good thing to bear in mind if you want to age gracefully.

Why Counting Your Breaths
Is Better than Counting Calories

Jean L. Kristeller and C. Brendan Hallett, from the psychology department at Indiana State University, investigated the efficacy of meditation for binge eating disorder (BED). Results suggest that meditation and mental training may be effective components in decreasing both frequency and severity of binge-eating episodes in persons with BED. Reported binges decreased to a quarter of what they were for people who undertook the meditation training.[9] When you have a sense of control over your impulses, all sorts of binges will decrease — so, yes, meditation can help you lose weight as well.

Faster Healing

Dr. Jon Kabat-Zinn and his colleagues from the University of Massachusetts published research in many journals, including the *American Journal of Psychiatry* and *Journal of Behavioral Medicine*, indicating that patients heal four times faster if they meditate; cancer patients who practiced meditation had significantly better emotional outlooks than a control group; and not only did meditation relieve symptoms in patients with anxiety and chronic pain but the benefits also continued for up to four years after training.[10] So it's not merely about keeping a positive outlook but, rather, getting the brain into a state where a positive outlook is natural. Health and well-being will follow.

Significant research has been conducted on meditation and its effects in many areas of life. As a result, increasing numbers of psychologists and physicians are incorporating it into their treatment regimes with great success. But why wait until we are sick? Mental resilience, including meditation, is a proven preventive and a way of creating lasting happiness.

Self-Awareness: Knowing Your Body

Mental Resilience Training focuses directly on the body. The goal in meditation is to become keenly aware of each and every one of your sensations. This can help you in many ways.

A simple example is being attuned to the feeling of fullness when you eat, which probably prevents overeating. (Of course, not all meditators are at their optimal weight, but for some, merely reducing calorie intake can be a significant achievement.)

Sensual Awareness

A common misperception is that meditators deprive themselves of sensory stimulus because they sit in a room without music, talking, or movement and are therefore denying themselves an important part of life. In fact, the opposite is true: meditators are generally more sensual and comfortable with the full range of sensory experiences than other people.

It is good to realize that, sometimes, decreasing sensory stimuli can be what a person needs. Normally we get so much stimulation that we cannot fully appreciate what we touch, eat, see, smell, or hear. Imagine going into a shop to find a perfume you like. By the time you get to the fourth or fifth perfume, you are so overloaded with input that your nose shuts down and nothing smells distinctive. This overload happens most of the time, in different ways, to all of our senses.

Ultimately it wears us out! However, through meditation you can shut out the daily bombardment (noise, TV, advertisements, all manner of sensory overload) and find mental quietness. When you are no longer inundated, you will be able to experience heightened pleasure from whatever engages your senses. So when you eat, you can focus your awareness on taste with much more precision. When you hug a loved one, your mental clarity allows you to enjoy every tender caress. You will be able to truly focus and enjoy all that your senses experience.

How Mental Resilience Training Enhances Your Love Life

We all know how to fall in love, but unfortunately not many of us know how to stay in love. Knowing how to listen is critical for staying connected and remaining in love. However, the mental chatter going around in our heads can make it difficult to focus on our partners. Also, heightened levels of clarity allow us to connect to our own emotions and our partners'. Practicing focus and clarity ensures that we keep love alive in our relationships.

Improved Listening Skills

Imagine that you have just joined your partner after a hard day's work looking after the kids or dealing with your boss, and you start a conversation. Your mind will likely still be processing information, decisions, and conversations from your day. You might get a glazed look in your eye, leading your partner to ask, "Are you really listening?"

The truth is, you're probably not. You aren't really present because you couldn't put down the thoughts wandering through your mind. Mental Resilience Training will increase your ability to listen with "unconditional presence, which is just being with what is, open and interested, without agenda."[11] This type of listening is very powerful. Your companion starts feeling connected to you, which opens up many avenues for the relationship to develop and deepen.

Emotional Awareness

Experienced meditators can pinpoint their emotions more immediately and accurately. Whatever they feel — whether joy, sadness, depression, or grief — they can understand and face with the appropriate intensity. Acknowledging all of your emotions (as opposed to denying or trying to numb them with too much comfort food or alcohol) is a sign of healthiness.

Emotional awareness means knowing when feelings are present in others and ourselves. This is obviously critical in relationships, especially when entering a new relationship. Most people start relationships with emotional baggage from previous relationships. Often we are not aware of the emotions that we carry around with us, and this can cause misunderstandings or defensiveness.

Through meditation we learn to notice, acknowledge, label,

and accept all of our emotions. As we become aware, we can stop carrying around what is no longer useful to us, and in letting such things go, we feel lighter and happier, and become easier to be around.

Mental Resilience Training has a number of benefits that can enhance your work, health, and relationships. Meditation helps you make fundamental and positive changes in your life, not through willpower, which can wax and wane, but through awareness. A meditation teacher offers the following reason for learning to meditate:

> *You can't make radical changes in the pattern of your life*
> *until you begin to see yourself exactly as you are now.*
> *As soon as you do that, changes flow naturally.*
> *You don't have to force or struggle or obey rules*
> *dictated to you by some authority. You just change.*
> *It is automatic.*
>
> GUNARATNA

There are so many times in our lives when we just cannot understand the right course of action. Sometimes we flit from one activity to another, without achieving anything in particular. We sometimes assume that if we keep doing various things, we will stumble onto the right path. Instead we often create more agitation and pain for ourselves.

The process of meditation can help us develop clarity about our decisions. Through this clarity, we develop our direction, which allows us to serve ourselves, our loved ones, and, ultimately, the world in an empowering way.

CHAPTER TWO

common misconceptions about meditation

I used to think that anyone doing anything weird was weird.
I suddenly realized that anyone weird wasn't weird at all
and that it was the people saying they were weird that were weird.

PAUL McCARTNEY

WHAT COMES TO MIND AT THE IDEA OF MEDITATION? Do you associate it with an attempt to reach a higher plane? Do you see an image of a bald man in orange robes sitting on a cold, stone monastery floor, chanting a mantra? Perhaps it's a picture of hippies with legs crossed in the lotus position, breathing deeply and murmuring, "Ommmmm."

Adding to the confusion is the fact that there are many different types of meditation practice — Transcendental Meditation (commonly known as TM), vipassana, zazen, stillness, or devotional meditation. Is each one different? Let's say that they all share many elements and each has its benefits, yet some would be more beneficial in certain contexts than others.

Meditation is becoming extraordinary at nothing special.

ZEN ADAGE

When discussing my personal meditation practice with friends and colleagues, I have encountered some misconceptions about precisely what meditation is or what it achieves. One particularly memorable instance came in response to my telling my boss that I meditate. "Ah," he ventured, "I don't meditate, because that's what cows do. I'm human, after all!" I'm still not sure what he thought cows really do. He was probably thinking more along the lines of rumination — hanging around all day, slowly chewing grass. Nevertheless, I am sure that cows are free of mental clutter, but they probably do not strive for the things that meditation offers: mental peace, mental resilience, and the skills to make better decisions in daily life.

Misconceptions can discourage people from beginning a meditation practice, or cause some to have unrealistic expectations about what meditation can provide. So, before describing the practical aspects of developing your own meditation practice, I'd like to address some of these misconceptions.

Misconception 1:
Meditation Is Only about Relaxation

You could think of meditation as practiced relaxation — the process of concentrating the mind, calming the body, and shutting out external stressors. These are key relaxation techniques and are also the first steps in any meditation practice.

But meditation is much more than relaxation. It enables you to delve deep inside yourself, into the subconscious and unconscious levels of your mind. Through this, you gain an awareness of what drives your actions and what underlies your decision-making processes. This state is often called *centeredness*. Simply, it means that your decisions come from awareness, not from transient mental clutter or, worse still, destructive emotions.

Problems cannot be solved at the same level of awareness
that created them.

ALBERT EINSTEIN

Misconception 2:
Meditation Means Going into a Trance

Meditation does not necessarily involve going into a trance state. It is not about zoning out, achieving unconsciousness, or escaping reality. In fact the opposite holds true — meditation is geared toward achieving a greater awareness of ourselves and our thinking processes.

Meditation is a more direct, raw experience of reality. When you meditate, you learn to acknowledge the internal chatter and focus on the precise emotions you are experiencing, thereby experiencing them with their full intensity.

When my daughter passed away, initially I was overwhelmed with grief and guilt. I just wanted to escape the dreadful pain of those emotions, so my first thought was to turn to alcohol and antidepressants. I feared facing my emotions and instead wanted to run away from them.

The process of running away from negative feelings toward positive ones is very tiring. Meditation provides you with the chance to sit with your emotions and actually *experience* them, a process that, initially, you may find challenging but, ultimately, extremely liberating and invigorating. Facing your emotions and acknowledging them gives you courage and strength. It provides mental stamina, or emotional resilience, to make decisions that are not adversely affected by your feelings. According to psychologist John Welwood, "Uncovering the raw energy of emotions is like moving into the depths of the oceans, underneath the whitecaps of emotional frenzy and the broader swells of feelings, where all remains calm."[1]

Misconception 3:
Meditation Is Just a Fad

A fad or trend that comes and goes does so because it usually lacks substance or can't demonstrate real results. It might deliver instant gratification, but it rarely requires a significant commitment of time or energy. On the other hand, meditation has been a cornerstone of Eastern philosophy for thousands of years. Although it has a shorter history of acceptance in mainstream Western society, it is increasingly recognized as a valid and effective tool. The health benefits are so significant that meditation is now recommended as an effective health regime for many — from executives, mothers, lawyers, and prison inmates to elite athletes and police officers, to name few.

Misconception 4:
Meditation Is Only for Holy People

The misconceptions abound: to meditate, you must be enlightened, become a vegetarian, join a religion or cult, or must avoid evil thoughts. Right? Wrong! Meditation is a practice of calm, focused thinking and attention that is available to, and effective for, everyone. It is for people like you and me who work every day and have to make decisions on what to buy or sell; whom to hire or fire, date, or marry; how to meet a tough deadline; or whether to say yes or no to that boring cocktail party. Meditation is for people who face the daily pressures of trying to balance work with healthy families and relationships. Meditation is suitable for vegetarians and nonvegetarians alike.

Misconception 5:
Meditation Makes You Spaced Out

Meditation became popular in the West in the 1960s; it arrived alongside experimentation with alternative lifestyles and drugs.

As a result, some assume that people who meditate also take drugs. Though meditation can make you feel naturally high or joyous, its effects are generally the opposite of those of taking drugs.

Drugs often make you lose touch with reality, numbing your experience of emotions. Meditation enables you to experience the reality of your emotions head on and simultaneously develop your ability to focus. The state of bliss achieved in meditation comes from having the courage to face an intense emotion and experience it in all its rawness.

I tend to experience this joyous feeling when my meditation contrasts with a negative experience just preceding it, such as an argument with my wife or barely meeting a brutally tight deadline. The more intense the prior emotion, the more blissful my meditation makes me feel, just as coming into an air-conditioned room on a hot day is more pleasurable the hotter it is outside.

Misconception 6:
Meditation Takes Up Too Much Time

A common complaint for many people is, "I already don't have enough time to do all I want to do, so how can I start another activity?" Many people considering meditation might be put off, fearing it will take up time that is already in short supply. However, the paradox is that meditation actually gives people more time.

My meditation teacher assured me that one minute of meditation is equivalent to ten minutes of deep sleep (however, I recommend that beginners start off with ten to fifteen minutes of meditation initially; this is enough to get you started); the deep rest you get in meditation actually helps clear your mind so that you become a more effective thinker. In turn, you will be able to make decisions faster and therefore have more time in your day.

In *The Seven Habits of Highly Effective People*, Stephen Covey uses the metaphor of "sharpening the saw" as a picture of how a focused mind creates time. By taking the time out to focus the mind, or sharpen the mental saw, you can cut through the decisions of life faster and in a more considered way.[2] With increased mental focus, the effective time you spend with your family or at work will increase in intensity and quality.

Misconception 7:
Meditation Requires Thinking about Nothing

This is the most common misconception I hear about meditation. People say to me, "I can't meditate, because I can't turn off my mind." However, especially for beginners, meditation is not about thinking of nothing. True, meditation is about slowing the mind, but it does not require that you empty it completely. In fact, trying to think of nothing actually makes you think of something. Try it! Meditation requires you to be *aware* of your thoughts and reactions. By focusing on the thinking process, the space between each thought will increase, your thinking will calm down, and you will relax.

Meditation helps you make peace with whatever is going on in your mind. As you become aware of and accept the mental chatter and stories you spin for yourself, you will develop the willpower and capacity to let them go.

As our society evolves, it gets more complex; the world gets louder, faster, and more demanding. Because meditation provides the skills to achieve a sense of calm and resilience, it will continue to attract more and more practitioners and advocates. Meditation is much more useful in the middle of mayhem than on the mountaintop.

CHAPTER THREE

meditation metaphors and models

We learn a lot of things,
but we don't learn how to deal with our inner life.

PAULE SALOMON

WHILE LEARNING MENTAL RESILIENCE TRAINING, you will likely wonder, "Am I doing this right?" Let me introduce you to some metaphors that may help you make sense of the question. If your meditation practice helps you identify with the following metaphors, you're doing it right.

The soul never thinks without a picture.

ARISTOTLE

Metaphor 1:
Clarity in a Glass of Muddy Water

Many meditation teachers liken the mind to a glass of clear water that you can see straight through. There are no obstructions; there is nothing clouding your view from one side of the glass to another.

Now imagine putting no more than a teaspoonful of dirt in that water and giving it a stir. What do you see? After just a bit of stirring, the water becomes so muddy that you can no longer see through it. The water is so murky, you couldn't see a light on the other side of the glass.

Now imagine that you've set down the glass of muddy water to allow the water and dirt to settle. As the turbulence stills, the elements begin to separate, and the water becomes less murky. The longer you leave it, the clearer the water becomes. Left for a couple of hours, your glass would have crystal-clear water at the top and sediment on the bottom.

This is very similar to the way the mind works. Stir it up, and it's hard to see much; let it settle, and there is clarity. The mud in the water represents the various challenges thrown at you daily.

Metaphor 1: Clarity in a Glass of Muddy Water

Imagine an extremely challenging day. Say you had a tiff with your partner before work. You have numerous deadlines looming and meetings to prepare for, your phone has been ringing off the hook since you got to the office, and your in-box is full of urgent emails you haven't had the chance to open. At this point, your mind is probably like the glass of dirty water, with flying thoughts clouding your vision. And if this dirty water represents your current state of mind, it's not truly a desirable standpoint for important decision making or effective action.

What does meditation do? Simply, meditation provides the same relief from the muddiness or confusion in your mind as allowing the glass of dirty water to settle. The challenges do not go away — the dirt is still in the glass — but it is settled, and you can see clearly.

Meditation is the process of keeping still, mentally and physically, which calms the mind and settles the mental chatter. If you train your mind to be still, then when it's time to make a decision, you can perceive all of the issues with clarity and determine how to resolve them in a very clear fashion. You will have created the mental bench strength to drop your mental chatter so that you can make a decision based on your true values rather than the myriad thoughts running amok in your mind.

The real voyage of discovery consists not in seeking new lands,
but in seeing with new eyes.

MARCEL PROUST

Metaphor 2:
Resilience — Holding a Box of Chocolates

Imagine holding a box of chocolates in your outstretched arm. It probably seems effortless until you imagine having to keep your arm outstretched for five minutes, holding the box. The longer you hold it, the more things change. Your arm probably starts to ache, and the box begins to feel heavy.

Metaphor 2: Resilience – Holding a Box of Chocolates

If you hold onto the box for another five or ten minutes, your arm will begin to burn with pain, and the box will feel heavier and heavier. You will probably want to put it down. Imagine doing that. Is it a relief?

Your next step is to rest your arm. Now imagine picking up the box again, but only after you've rested. This time, the box probably doesn't feel heavy at all. Your arm likely feels much more resilient than it did previously, even though the weight of the box never actually changes; your perception of it is different now than when you had to hold onto it for a longer time. It was the act of holding onto the box that required all the effort.

Consider this: the box of chocolates represents your thoughts.

If you're thinking a thought for a brief time, it won't necessarily weigh you down or give you pain. But hold a thought, particularly a negative one, in your mind, mulling it over and over, and the result will be very different. Obsessive thinking, when thoughts stay stuck in your mind, can build its own momentum, whether the problem is how to have that difficult conversation with your loved one, improve productivity before the next board meeting, deal with somebody who cheated you, or fire a team member. Such thoughts are persistent. You think them in the shower, at work, while driving, or when trying to get to sleep. It becomes exhausting; the more you hold such thoughts in your mind, the more tired you get.

Meditation gives you the same relief from such pervasive thoughts as that of resting your arm when it began to ache. Meditation gives you the discipline, the mental bench strength, to put your thoughts aside, down, or on hold. When your mind is rested, you will be better equipped to resolve the negative issues and will find that your mind is more resilient. You will make decisions from a true understanding of the issues, rather than out of mental exhaustion or attempts to chase the noise away.

A mind that is strong enough to let go of thoughts is less likely to allow thoughts that cause suffering in the form of depression, anxiety, or other negative states.

Metaphor 3: Natural Radiance — The Joy of Life Revealed on a Blank Screen

Imagine that your mind is a projection screen and the story being projected onto it runs nonstop. The images (your thoughts) flicker endlessly, to the extent that it's hard to imagine the screen behind the images. However, when you stop the movie, you notice the screen. It is obvious, clear, and radiant, without any images on it.

Each of us plays out our stories on our mental screens, and of course, those stories seem supremely important. The characters, events, and emotions seem very real and significant.

But when we stop the projection, the continuous flicker of our own invention, we suddenly see the blank screen behind it. This lack of activity (of story) leads to a quietness of mind, a contented state. The contentedness stems from the knowledge that you can be at peace just by being yourself, without any conspicuous signs of success, such as the promotion, the bonus, the expensive holidays, or the perfect relationship.

Think of your spirit as the blank screen — uncontaminated, pure, and joyous. This represents the essence of each human being. Meditation allows you to access this clean screen, and knowing this is the basis of contentment.

Metaphor 4:
Power — Developing Mental Muscles

Imagine that you have an ongoing problem and, in the course of your day, you think about it over and over. In doing so, you create a neural pathway in your brain, and by repeating the thought, you follow the same pathway over and over again. Each time the thought recurs, it needs less and less effort to follow the established path. Now imagine that this thought is a tire going over and over a muddy track. With repeated driving on this track, the tire carves out a rut. Eventually it becomes very hard to steer the wheel out of the rut.

Because meditation helps you develop a strong and resilient mind with strong mental muscles, you will be able to get that particularly stuck thought out of that rut without a great deal of effort. Meditation enables you to get out of tight corners and discard thoughts that are not beneficial for you. Imagine the thrill when you can instruct the mind to no longer think a certain thought.

A strong mind is a mind that does not suffer from boredom,
frustration, depression, or unhappiness.
It has learned to drop what it doesn't want.
Meditation practice has given it the necessary muscles.

AYYA KHEMA

Life should be lived intensely and joyously. Ultimately your meditation will allow you to do just that. The metaphors in this chapter are aimed at helping you in your Mental Resilience Training. Through the practices outlined in this book and the accompanying audio, you will gain clarity and resilience. You will also develop a greater awareness of your own natural state of mental radiance while developing your mental muscles.

CHAPTER FOUR

a model of the mind

As the soil, however rich it may be,
cannot be productive without cultivation,
so the mind without culture can never produce good fruit.

SENECA

AS YOU BEGIN TO MEDITATE, it is useful to have a model of the mind that will help paint a picture of what you may encounter. However, as industrial statistician George Box said, "All models are wrong; some models are useful." As quantum physicists, behaviorists, psychiatrists, psychologists, and neurosurgeons continue advancing their fields, they produce new understandings and evolve new models of the mind. This model is one that my meditation students and I have found particularly useful.

I use the analogy of computer and digital technology, and in this model there are four parts that make up the mind.

- The conscious mind (a computer's memory chip)
- The subconscious mind (a computer's hard drive)
- The personal unconscious mind (the office computer network)
- The collective (or universal) unconscious mind (the Internet)

In our daily lives, we access information, intelligence, or experiences from these sources, sometimes by design but often by accident. The meditation techniques in this book will help you become more aware of the source of your information, emotions, insight, and wisdom.

The Conscious Mind

The conscious mind manages our daily functioning. This is the level at which you experience conscious perceptions, thoughts, and feelings. Here, you remember where you put the keys, how to get to work, or that you have to call your mother. Though a multitude of activities can be recalled or planned, this state of mind represents a very small component of your total mental capacity.

When you receive a stimulus with the conscious mind, you are aware of the stimulus and how it affects you. For example, if somebody asked you where you were last night, you could tell them accurately where you went, what you did, how you got there, and also how you felt at that time. You will have the information about each element of the experience, but one of the major purposes of the conscious mind is to filter the stimuli you receive so that you are not overburdened with that information.

Using the computer analogy, I like to describe the conscious mind as the memory chip (RAM) of your consciousness. Although it's comparatively small, it handles the roaring traffic of thoughts coming in and out.

The Subconscious Mind

The subconscious mind is larger than the conscious mind and holds your entire personal history. It has an extraordinary capacity to store a memory of each and every thing that ever happened to you and that you felt or thought — memories of your first day at school, the song that was playing the first time you kissed somebody, the smell of your mother when she first held you in her arms.

The subconscious mind takes in information without your conscious direction. It creates a magnificent, rich storehouse of impressions. When you hear a song that you last heard in high school, feelings and emotions well up from that time of your life. Many emotional triggers reside in this part of the mind, and though you are not conscious of them, they influence you deeply. Sometimes we feel agitated or stressed by something indefinable, but we have difficulty pulling all of the details of that past experience from our subconscious.

If somebody asked what you did last night and you were able to fully access the subconscious, you could recall a vast amount of information. You could remember the color of all the cars you passed on the way to your destination, all the different aftershaves and perfumes of the people you met, and how many steps you took to your destination. The subconscious would have stored how you felt when greeted by each person you encountered. The subconscious mind keeps all this information and more, and uses it in specific ways to affect your decision making.[1]

Your intuitive ability is based on your capacity to access and decipher information stored in your subconscious. Consider a time when, despite having read all the facts and figures, your intuition told you to do something that went against those facts. Here, your subconscious mind was active, providing insight and delivering a subliminal message based on all the information it collected in the past. Past incidents may affect your decision making concerning many things in the present, from relationships to careers. For example, perhaps there was an incident in your childhood that made you feel distressed or inadequate. That incident, though not consciously in your thoughts or memories, may still drive how you react today. The subconscious mind exerts immense power on our decision-making mind.

> *The intuitive mind is a sacred gift, and the rational mind*
> *is a faithful servant. We have created a society*
> *that honors the servant and has forgotten the gift.*
>
> ALBERT EINSTEIN

Turning to our computer model, the subconscious is the hard drive of the mind. It is much larger than the RAM portion, and it's very powerful because it stores the memory of everything you have consciously seen, heard, felt, or sensed in your life. It stores all of the programs that you use to give meaning to different events occurring in your life. By *programs*, I mean the rules that your mind assigns to yourself and others.

The Personal Unconscious Mind

The third part of the mind, the personal unconscious mind, regulates your functions and stores your life information, even when the conscious mind is not aware that it's necessary. By definition, the personal unconscious mind is part of the subconscious mind, because it is below, or *sub-*, the conscious mind.

Consider the fact that most of your bodily processes are not consciously controlled. Your heart pumps blood, your lungs breathe in and out, and your other vital organs function regularly, all of which are incredibly complex tasks. The many millions of stimuli that course through our bodies daily are mostly unconscious; for example, immediately after eating, we unconsciously start the process of digesting and assimilating nutrients.

You do not have to be conscious of information for it to

enter your unconscious mind. In *Vital Lies, Simple Truths: The Psychology of Self-Deception*, psychologist Daniel Goleman writes that some patients under deep anesthesia in the operating room could remember the conversations doctors had with them while they were unconscious.[2] This means that even though the conscious mind was asleep, the unconscious mind was still working and registering information. (For more information, refer to the work of psychologist Henry Bennett at the University of California Medical Center at Davis.[3])

The unconscious possesses memory and skills that we need not consciously recall for performing an action. For example, once we have learned how, we no longer consciously control the motions of driving a car or playing a sport. Some people take unconscious skills to extraordinary levels. Some autistic savants can tell the precise time — to the second — without having to look at a clock.[4] Others can tell the specific measurements of an object — to within a fraction of an inch — just by glancing at it, while others can draw spectacularly detailed and accurate representations of buildings without having spent a great deal of time studying or observing them. Some have the ability to count and remember cards with such precision and speed that they would rival the best calculators.

These individuals were not taught these skills. Nor did they actively train their conscious minds to learn them. They accessed the power of their unconscious minds. Researchers now suggest that ordinary people are capable of performing such feats, which, ironically, may be possible by turning *off* certain parts of our brains![5] In other words, by stopping the conscious mind from filtering out information, and by directly accessing the unconscious mind, we may increase our ability to capture and analyze information.

Many of your dormant thoughts, from banal details to

creative ideas, live in your unconscious mind. It is the home of your intuition, or sixth sense. You may have experienced its power when you had a strange sensation that something was awry without necessarily being able to identify the cause or even confirm a result. (Well aware of the power of appealing to hidden fears or secret desires, marketing strategists develop subliminal messages to achieve targeted behavior. They appeal to the fears or desires buried in the subconscious mind.)

Sometimes you feel a niggling doubt as you walk out of the house. You can't pinpoint the reason, but you know something is not right. For many people, the sensation is centered in their stomachs. Something makes you turn around, and sure enough, you find that you left the iron on or the back door open. Where did this knowledge come from? What sparked it off? If you had consciously thought about it, you might not have been able to remember what was wrong, but unconsciously your body was sent a signal that you responded to.

A warning or foreknowing sensation might last longer than a small niggling feeling. Generally feelings that linger are indicative of some past event, usually one associated with emotional pain. The sensation is trying to tell you something, but you may not have the right tools to decipher the message. Though you are not conscious of the reason behind the sensation, it will influence your behavior; for example, you may try to mask negative feelings or search for ways to create positive ones.

All memory is unconscious, and remembering something means bringing the information stored outside the conscious mind into conscious awareness. Because memory is vital for both thinking and learning, the unconscious is an extremely important part of your psyche.

The personal unconscious is the home of creativity and inspiration. Your unconscious processes cannot be made conscious at will; their unraveling requires the use of specific techniques, such as meditation. So accessing this mind is a crucial step to fully realizing your capabilities; enhancing your daily creative output; and making informed, effective decisions.

I think of this part of the mind as the computer network in an office or organization. Each machine receives information and programs, whether or not the individual computers are turned on; the network remains aware of a connection between it and each member.

The Collective Unconscious Mind

The collective unconscious does not owe its existence to personal experience and is not a personal acquisition. The contents of the collective unconscious have never been in consciousness and therefore have never been individually acquired.

The collective unconscious is universal. It cannot be developed through individual experiences, as is the personal unconscious; rather, the collective unconscious predates the individual. It is the repository of what Carl Jung called *archetypes*, universal symbols (religious, spiritual, and mythological) that all humans share. This part of the mind contains the intelligence of our entire human existence. This intelligence derived from our species is the part of the mind that records our human journey. From a cellular level, this is the intelligence of DNA; it allows cells to replicate and wounds to heal. On a macro level, the collective unconscious contains the universal stories from different parts of the world and from all cultures, attesting to the existence of a shared consciousness.

Mystics from many different backgrounds describe the sense of being connected to this repository of knowledge, and their descriptions are quite similar. For the purposes of this book and your

Mental Resilience Training, it is sufficient to say that the collective unconscious exists and you can access it. However, I would stress that believing in its existence is not a prerequisite for you to benefit from meditation.

I compare this part of the mind to the Internet, which is vast and diverse, and can link to almost limitless sources of knowledge. We can individually access the information of the Internet using our personal computers; however, we weren't necessarily the ones who placed the information there. Yet, with the right connection, we can access this storehouse of knowledge anytime.

> *The intellect has little to do on the road to discovery.*
> *There comes a leap in consciousness;*
> *call it intuition or what you will — the solution comes to you*
> *and you don't know how or why.*
>
> ALBERT EINSTEIN

Gateways between Different Parts of the Mind

Until you are comfortable with your meditation practice, you may feel that the potentials presented for the different states of the mind sound too far fetched, even impossible. Consider this: if you hadn't done any training, yet were contemplating an Olympic marathon, you might deem such a feat impossible to achieve at the outset of your adventure. Indeed, you might not want to run the Olympic marathon after all; maybe you would prefer to go out for a daily jog. You run because it makes you feel good and keeps you healthy.

The same idea applies to Mental Resilience Training. You can access and experience the various levels of consciousness if you want, and to whatever depth you desire. Many meditators who are able to access the deeper parts of their minds have developed their mental muscles because they have undertaken the necessary training. You might even call them mental Olympians. Such an achievement might begin slowly, but it's still within your grasp.

Now that you have an understanding of the various levels of the psyche and the richness of experiences that you can access, you may want to know exactly how it happens! The different parts of the mind are connected by a series of gateways, which are very tight most of the time, prohibiting very much information from flowing between them. However, as we relax, each gateway enlarges, opening up more and more space for information to be transmitted.

Sometimes the gateways open extremely easily, almost incidentally. Say you run into someone you recognize at a party but can't, for the life of you, remember the person's name. However, the next day, when you are driving, bathing, or playing your flute, the name pops into your mind out of the blue!

As you relaxed, the gateway between the conscious and subconscious minds opened up, allowing you to access a piece of information that wasn't previously available to you. You hadn't forgotten the name; you were merely unable to recall it on cue.

The key to opening up your mind's gateways is to have control over your brain waves. As you begin to meditate and relax more deeply, the gateways open up between the different types of mind. This happens because your brain emits different brain-wave patterns.

Types of Brain Waves

For the purposes of your meditation practice, it's important to understand four types of brain waves, indicating a range from most to least activity. This is not a detailed anatomical explanation but should give you a basic understanding.[6]

Beta Waves

When aroused and very active, the brain generates beta waves. Beta waves are of relatively low amplitude yet, at 15 to 40 cycles per second, are the fastest of the four different brain waves. A couple engaged in an argument, a person feeling stressed over a missed deadline, a student experiencing pre-exam stress, and a parent irritated by a crying child would exhibit beta waves.

Alpha Waves

Alpha waves represent the amount of brain activity in a relaxed state. Alpha waves are slower than beta and higher in amplitude. They range from 9 to 14 cycles per second. A businessperson settling down to relax after a presentation at a major conference would most likely exhibit alpha waves. So would a parent relaxing with a favorite novel after putting a crying toddler to bed.

Theta Waves

Theta waves are even higher in amplitude and slower in frequency than alpha waves, at 5 to 8 cycles per second. You will probably exhibit theta waves if you start visualizing the vacation you plan to go on in a few weeks. While driving on a long trip and letting your mind wander (even while being alert to road conditions), you may start experiencing the theta state. Many people experience theta waves while enjoying a long, luxurious bath.

When we sink into the theta state, we access more-creative parts of the mind, which can take many complex ideas, theories, and data and turn them into a revelation. One of the best-known revelations that occurred in this state was Archimedes' discovery (and subsequent shrieks of "Eureka!") of the principles of displacement of water, which is the basis of boat design. Both

Leonardo da Vinci and Michelangelo were rumored to spend much of their time in a daydream state, presumably accessing the more creative parts of their minds.[7]

Delta Waves

Delta brain waves have the greatest amplitude of all four states and the slowest frequency, at approximately 1.5 to 4 cycles per second. If your brain activity were zero, you would be brain dead. If your brain activity during very deep, dreamless sleep were measured, your brain waves would be approximately 2 to 3 cycles per second.

Someone in a deep meditative state could have a significant proportion of alpha, delta, and theta waves, but only some beta waves. Different forms of meditation practice result in different brain-wave patterns, indicating which parts of the mind the practitioner is accessing.

As we continue meditation practice, we will emit different brain-wave patterns, meaning that we will access different parts of our minds as the gateways open up. This may result in the rise of surprising thoughts, because we will be unaware of how they have entered into our minds. The key here is to just observe such thoughts and let them go. Our meditation is not putting these thoughts into our minds.

One of the benefits of meditation is that we will become more adept at entering into the alpha, theta, and delta states. When the brain emits these wave patterns, it is capable of high levels of creativity and deep rest.

As we go deeper into meditation, we start opening the parts of our minds from which we derive our insights and wisdom. With the appropriate training we can access every part of our minds.

Although these examples of various states of brain activity range from quite agitated to deep, dreamless sleep, the four types of brain waves exist in our brain all the time but at different ratios. Different brain-wave patterns allow us to access different parts of the mind, because the differing proportions of beta, alpha, theta, and delta waves correlate to different mental and meditative states.

PART TWO

practice

*Mental resilience is 98 percent practice
and 2 percent theory.*

NANDA

CHAPTER FIVE

getting started

I see my path, but I don't know where it leads.
Not knowing where I'm going is what inspires me to travel it.

ROSALIA DE CASTRO

THE PRACTICE I TEACH has been used for many years by warriors and monks — warriors, because they want concentrated
focus for the heat of battle. For warriors, distraction could ultimately result in death. While you are not a warrior, sometimes
we all need that absolute focus — whether at work or in a relationship — when we need to give our undivided attention to
somebody who truly needs to be heard. Monks also learned this
technique, because they wanted to experience deep levels of peace,
fulfillment, and ultimate reality. Once again, you may not be a
monk, but at some level, aren't we all looking for that inner peace
that eludes us? Because I have been lucky to study all the major religions, I have drawn from all traditions. However, the yoga practiced by my teacher is the foundation of Mental Resilience
Training.

Creating a Meditation Space

Choose a meditation area in your home or at work that can become a sanctuary from the hustle and bustle of life. Your special spot can be as simple as a cushion or a chair in a corner of the room. (After a few days of practice, just experiencing these triggers will allow you to unwind!)

I suggest you create the sanctuary by adding some olfactory cues as well; have aromatic oils in an oil burner, light some incense, or place something close to the space to create a special, appealing atmosphere. (However, burning incense in an office is almost always prohibited and could easily trigger the building's automatic smoke detectors and sprinklers!) Smell is a very evocative sense that can swiftly affect one's mood and brain activity. Creating a regular location, enhanced by special surrounds and smells isn't mandatory, but it can provide a cue for your mind to quiet down.

Most of the distractions you will encounter when meditating, many of which will be beyond your control, will come from your surroundings. If you start meditating in a noisy location, you may struggle to concentrate. You could be drawn to the shriek of a car alarm, laughter from somewhere in the office, or an unexpected knock at the door. However, you can take steps to minimize the potential distractions.

Try to find a meeting room or office where you can switch off the phone. At home, avoid using your bed as your meditation spot, because lying on the bed might cue you to start dozing, rendering you unable to realize the full benefits of meditation.

As you become more proficient, you can meditate anywhere. I have many students who meditate on trains and planes. After more practice, you can go into meditative states even while waiting for the walk sign at traffic lights.

Preparing to Meditate

Preparation is an important part of meditation practice. Just as you would need to stretch before running or doing any physical exercise, you need to prepare for meditation practice.

You will need some practice switching off your mind from what you were doing before time to meditate. It is difficult to switch from a hard day's work at the office or looking after the family to suddenly sitting down for meditation. You will need to slow down gradually. So, how do you get started? A few simple techniques can make all the difference to the effectiveness and speed of your meditation preparation.

Taking a Walk

A walk will help you to enter into a calm state. As you walk, focus on your breath. I tell my students to try a five-minute walk, inhaling for three steps and exhaling for four steps. If you consistently make your exhalation longer than your inhalation, you will feel calmer. If you feel a bit flat or tired, instead make your inhalation longer, inhaling for four steps and exhaling for three steps.

Enjoying a Bath or Shower

Taking a bath will certainly relax you. Make it as leisurely as possible.

Eating or Drinking Slowly

Eating slowly will engage your senses, helping you slow down. By deliberately dwelling on the taste of the food or drink — feeling its texture, listening to your chewing, and smelling the flavors — you will help yourself prepare for your meditation.

Stretching with Yoga or Pilates

Yoga and Pilates are two physical therapies that combine bodily exercise with a focus on your breath, thereby engaging your parasympathetic nervous system, which facilitates relaxation. This can really help get you into the mental frame to start meditation. (See chapter 7 for a more detailed explanation of the parasympathetic nervous system.)

Finding a Good Posture

Posture is critical in meditation. Your posture should support the body, keeping it still so you can allow the mind to settle. Each person will need to find his or her ideal posture; for some, it is sitting cross-legged and, for others, upright in a sturdy chair. When you start meditating, make sure to be aware of your posture and develop the right position from the beginning.

Posture: A Skillful Way

As you sit, you will feel aches and pains. These will pass, but it is important to make sure that you can sit for at least twenty minutes to an hour in your chosen posture. This helps the mind achieve stillness.

Good posture in meditation involves gaining support from your skeleton, not your muscles. So, as your muscles relax, the gravitational pull on your body grounds you. The idea is to get into a position where your bones actually support your physical structure. Be patient; it has taken me some time to develop a posture I feel comfortable with. Following are some guiding principles.

Posture: A Skillful Way

Adjust the height of your hips and knees. Your knees should be slightly below the line of your buttocks, your pelvis should lean slightly forward, and your back should be straight. The first thing to consider is the cushion or chair height, which should give you the right proportions of support so that you can lean forward slightly. Your pelvis, hips, and knees should create a triangle, which will provide a stable base.

You may choose to sit on a chair or a cushion, or even use folded towels that you can build up to the necessary height for a comfortable posture. Whatever you use, ensure that your sitting bones are in touch with the hard surface of the cushion. To do that, it can be useful to grab the cheeks of your buttocks and separate them to allow your sitting bones contact with the surface of the cushion or chair.

Place your hands in a comfortable position. There is no ideal position for your hands, except that you should ensure that they are supported. You may place them palm up on your thighs, palm down on your knees, or in front of you, clasped or open; do whatever feels comfortable. Some traditions state that certain hand positions are better than others; however, I feel that this is a personal preference. You may find that on some days you may wish to clasp your hands, while on others, you may want to keep them on your hips. There is no "one size fits all." Become aware of your feelings, and you will naturally gravitate to the position that suits you best.

Adjust your shoulders and back. If you sit in front of a computer or drive a car for extended periods, or do anything that makes you hunch over and round your shoulders, you will need to correct this posture for meditation. It is important to position your shoulders correctly to get the right amount of air into your lungs.

Try to relax your shoulders and push them back so that your sternum opens, allowing you to breathe deeply. Avoid excessively arching your back, which leads to lower back strain. Slouching will make you tired and even sleepy. Experiment as much as you can, until your shoulder positions feel right. When you start a session, try to hold your posture until the end of the session; avoid adjusting it during the meditation. If you need to make adjustments, do so between sessions.

Posture: An Unskillful Way

Leaning forward leads to back pain.

Leaning back leads to shortness of breath.

Align your neck. Did you ever see the old movies that show young girls practicing walking with books balanced on their heads? Your neck should be just as aligned and relaxed as that! Try to make sure that, while you are seated, your head aligns with your spine, with your neck relaxed. You may even want to practice with a book on your head. If you can balance the book, your head is balanced on your spine. It's crucial to keep that balance so that, as you sit longer and longer, there will be no strain on your neck muscles.

Posture: An Aligned Neck

Scheduling Your Session

The time you choose should be comfortable for you and obviously should fit your daily schedule. I find the morning a particularly good time to meditate because my head is clear of most thoughts at that time.

You may consider showering prior to sitting, because it will wake you up, providing you a clearer session. Once your practice is established, meditation in the morning generally ensures a sense of tranquility for the rest of the day.

The other good time to meditate is directly after getting home from work, before starting your evening activities. I find that couples who meditate immediately after work communicate better after their sessions. The meditation allows them to relax and release the clutter of daily activity that might otherwise intervene in their relationship.

Try not to meditate after a big meal, because your body's digestion process is at work, which may make you feel sleepy.

Duration and Frequency of Meditation

There is no general rule for duration and frequency of meditation, other than to try to establish a rhythm. Try to sit at least once a day, at the same time each day. Begin with five minutes of meditation a day. Then add five minutes each week until you can manage thirty minutes a day. Many of my students comment on how long it feels to sit for ten minutes. But after a twenty-one-day course, their sense of time changes, their enjoyment of the process increases, and many find they want to sit for longer and longer periods because of what they experience.

Try not to miss a session. Even if you sit for just one minute (instead of your usual amount), that is an achievement. After a concerted effort of just three weeks, you will notice a very healthy habit forming. Even if you have to miss a session (perhaps for a meeting or dinner) at your scheduled time, make an effort to remember it by taking a deep breath and affirming that this is your meditation time.

Getting the basics right will help take away many of the obstacles that face new meditators. You can create a simple checklist such as the one on the next page to make sure you get started in the right direction for each Mental Resilience Training session.

The main rule is to enjoy it! Experiment to find the length, schedule, and space for your meditation. Try to treat it like a hobby, not an obligation. Make it into a special time for you to just be yourself.

Meditation Preparation Checklist

Preparing Yourself

- ❏ Take off your jacket.
- ❏ Remove or loosen your tie or scarf.
- ❏ Remove or loosen your belt.
- ❏ Untie your hair.
- ❏ Remove your glasses.
- ❏ Take off your watch.
- ❏ Remove your shoes and socks or stockings.

Preparing Your Space

- ❏ Minimize the possibility of disturbances (close the door, find a quiet place, cancel any meetings).
- ❏ Close the windows and draw the blinds if necessary.
- ❏ Turn off all phones.
- ❏ Turn off all computers, PDAs, and other electronic devices.

Adjusting Your Posture

- ❏ Straighten and relax your back.
- ❏ Balance your head on your neck.
- ❏ Position your knees lower than the hips.
- ❏ Support your hands.
- ❏ Tilt your hips forward.

CHAPTER SIX

the stages of meditation

It does not matter how slowly you go,
so long as you do not stop.

CONFUCIUS

MEDITATION HAS A NUMBER OF STAGES. Most people give up on meditation because they believe that they cannot sit still and focus their minds. Let's face it, coming in after a hard day's work at the office or looking after the kids, you can't just plop down and hope to still the mind. You must take intermediate steps. Mental Resilience Training ensures that you build a foundation so that you gradually reach a stage where you feel comfortable sitting still for fifteen minutes. Without the foundation stages, people give up prematurely and therefore do not experience the full benefits of the practice.

The summary below provides some context as you embark on your journey. Later in the book, you will find more-precise instructions with in-depth explanations of each concept or practice. There you will find a step-by-step breakdown of how to gain mastery of each stage. Also, in chapter 12 you will find a twenty-one-day plan for turning meditation into a very constructive habit.

However, if you want to dive straight in, feel free to read chapter 12 now and use the guided Mental Resilience Training in the accompanying audio.

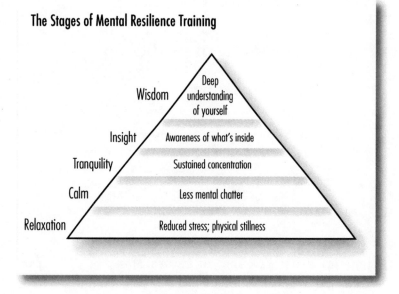

The Stages of Mental Resilience Training

Wisdom — Deep understanding of yourself

Insight — Awareness of what's inside

Tranquility — Sustained concentration

Calm — Less mental chatter

Relaxation — Reduced stress; physical stillness

1. Relaxation — The first stage of training is about relaxation. Relaxation is the entry point. There is no way you can actually embark on the journey of meditation without first experiencing relaxation. When you relax, you enjoy physical stillness and a lowered stress level.

2. Meditative Calm — The second stage of training is a feeling of calm. Calm reduces the noise or continual chatter of the stories that go around and around in your head. It takes a few seconds to become aware of all the mental chatter; just close your eyes and observe your breath going in and out, and the awareness of your breath will allow the noise to

diminish, resulting in a new sense within you — one of calm.

3. Emotional Tranquility — The third stage of training, emotional tranquility, is achieved when, despite a level of mental chatter, you can maintain some measure of sustained concentration. Experiencing tranquility during meditation reenergizes the mind.

4. Insight — The fourth stage of training is insight, which means developing an understanding of the nature of what's inside you, an understanding of the feelings, fears, and aspirations that drive you.

5. Wisdom — This last stage, wisdom, is the highest level of meditation and brings with it a deep and profound understanding of yourself.

Unfortunately sometimes we choose poor substitutes for meditation. So when our bodies require relaxation we zone out in front of the TV. When we want to calm down, we down a couple of drinks to "calm the nerves."

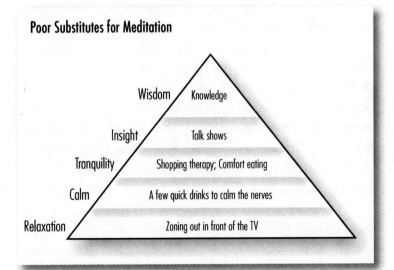

Poor Substitutes for Meditation

Wisdom / Knowledge

Insight / Talk shows

Tranquility / Shopping therapy; Comfort eating

Calm / A few quick drinks to calm the nerves

Relaxation / Zoning out in front of the TV

When we feel emotionally agitated we go on shopping sprees or indulge in comfort foods to calm our emotions. When we want insight we listen to or watch talk shows to learn from other people's attempts to gain insight. And last we choose knowledge over wisdom, which initially can feel the same but does not have the same level of personal connectedness.

Frequently Asked Questions

What will I experience as a beginner? Naturally the experience of meditation practice varies from one person to another. Some people feel a sense of calm almost straightaway. Some people feel a sense of detachment from problems, even though their problems still exist; however, once they start meditating regularly, their attitudes change toward the same formerly troublesome issues. Some people report that they start viewing their problems as if watching something on TV. This sense of detachment, or equanimity, is something we will cover later. Some people experience stress reduction and feelings of wellness, joy, and lightness even in their first few sessions.

However, it is worth noting that some students feel agitated when they begin meditating. If this happens to you, do not be alarmed. It generally passes within the first few sessions. It happens because people begin to listen to the constant chatter in their minds, which can be distressing. While they may previously have been aware of a general sense of unease or discontentment, they did not question their lives too deeply. Now, with meditation they become aware of their thoughts, which can be confronting.

Most students experience improved sleep patterns. In some cases students have reported vivid dreams. The reason for this is that as you meditate, the gateway opens up between your subconscious and conscious minds, allowing thoughts to surface during sleep.

Sometimes you may hear your stomach rumbling as you meditate; you may even start salivating. This signals that your digestive system is doing its work! As we relax, more blood is released into the digestive system than when we were tense. Some students get slightly sexually aroused, another consequence of increased blood flow in the body, this time to the sexual region.

Do not be distressed if you have any of these experiences. Just keep on sitting, and you will gradually experience greater levels of clarity.

How do I handle this infestation of fleas? When you start meditating you will notice how hard it is to stop fidgeting. You invariably will start getting the urge to scratch your nose, head, or legs, which can be very frustrating. One of my students said that an army of fleas was stalking him. The best thing to do is *not* respond to the itch; just become aware of it and let it pass. Unfortunately, if you start reacting to that urge, it will not go away. If you notice it and refrain from responding, it will pass and leave you with a sense of calm.

Personal Encounters with Meditation

Here is a typical beginner's meditation, according to Kate: "I sat down; I felt a bit restless. I had had a really tough day at work. I started focusing on counting my breaths.

"By the fourth breath, I started planning what I really needed to do the next day. I don't know how long it took for me to come back to focusing on my breath. Then I started again. This time I did not even get to the fourth breath. I thought, 'Wow, I have a great idea for my next vacation. If only I had a piece of paper next to me, I could write it down.'

"Then I realized I was planning, so I labeled my thoughts *planning* and came back to my breath. Then I started feeling sleepy. I thought, 'I really need to get some rest.' Then I started thinking about how I could redecorate my bedroom. Then I panicked because I needed to get to the mall for the sale on bedsheets. Then I started thinking that I had to find my driver's license because it was due for renewal.

"By that time, I got annoyed with myself for not meditating. I thought, 'I am so hopeless at this meditation thing.'

"I then made a real effort. I focused on my breath. I started feeling really light after a few breaths. I continued for what seemed an eternity, just focusing on my breath. I thought a couple of times, 'I must have forgotten to turn on the alarm clock to get me out of this meditation session.' I was sure I had been sitting for thirty minutes or longer. I waited a little while longer, almost willing the alarm to tell me that the session was over. I kept concentrating on my breath. Finally the alarm went off.

"When I opened my eyes, it had been only ten minutes."

Mental Resilience Training has five major stages; namely, relaxation, meditative calm, emotional tranquility, insight, and wisdom. These build upon each other so that you can develop your mental resilience progressively. As you move through each of the stages, you will prepare yourself for the next phase. The first stage that we will journey through is relaxation, a vital stage because it's the beginning of the journey. In this stage you will learn how to be physically still. As you learn how to totally relax, you will seek more opportunities to incorporate meditation into your life.

CHAPTER SEVEN

developing a relaxed state of mind

But do not distress yourself with imaginings.
Many fears are born of fatigue and loneliness.
Beyond a wholesome discipline, be gentle with yourself.

MAX EHRMANN

DO YOU STILL FEEL REALLY TIRED on getting out of bed after a
night's sleep? If you're tired before the day has actually started,
you didn't really rest or relax. You may think that relaxing is
something you do after you've done your work, had your conversations, or accomplished something in your day. It's what you
might do after everything else. But consider this: the most effective relaxed state is when your mind and body are still. From all
the research into the health benefits of relaxation, we know that
the more relaxed you are, the more effective you can be. The ability to relax is critical to conserving energy and working at your
optimal level. Unfortunately many people do not make time each
day to experience complete relaxation.

Being relaxed will certainly make a difference in how you feel
within yourself, but it is also a significant factor in how others respond to you. For example, if you feel tense before starting a conversation with someone, it is very likely that the other person will

feed off that tension as well. If both parties are tense you probably won't get the desired outcome for either of you.

Good Stress and Bad Stress

We know that physical and mental stress is part of life, and certainly part of doing business today. We continually push our minds and bodies to perform at high levels. It is important to remember that there are two types of stress: a positive stress, eustress; and a negative stress, distress.[1]

Eustress is driven by positive emotions or events, and produces a bodily response that leads to higher rates of attention or concentration. If you are about to play a sport at a competitive level or begin an exam for which you are well prepared, you will experience eustress. However, its evil cousin, distress, stimulates negative reactions. If you're experiencing long-term distress, it will manifest physically; perhaps you will experience it initially as tightness around the shoulders, persistent headaches, or even an inability to sleep properly. If you're experiencing these symptoms of distress (for example, you often feel as if you've been run over by a truck on arriving at work after a good night's rest), you may be at risk for a stress-related illness and should seriously consider how to bring relaxation into your life.

Research at the Mind/Body Medical Institute at Harvard University shows that 60 to 90 percent of all visits to medical providers in the United States are for stress-related disorders.

Understanding Relaxation

Relaxation is generally defined as a refreshment of body or mind, a meaning you are probably familiar with. However, I prefer a definition that comes from physics: "The return or adjustment of a system to equilibrium, following displacement or abrupt change."[2] Because change is inescapable, things and circumstances around us — from finances to relationships to health — change continually. In this state of flux, we must continually return to equilibrium. If we don't, we feel negative stress, which can lead to anxiety and depression.

Relaxation means different things to different people. Some find being in front of the TV or having a drink relaxing, but even while sitting around watching TV, you can still carry significant tension in your body. The next time you watch the TV news, notice how your body feels when you hear about a suicide bomber or an economist predicting a coming recession. Chances are, such news will make your body contract in some way (very noticeably or imperceptibly), and your breathing will most probably become more rapid.

For some people, relaxation might mean walking in nature or reading for pleasure. While these activities might seem to release the mind from its usual chores, they do not actually relax the mind. Rather, these activities only distract the mind and, once they're over, leave you without much refreshment or equilibrium.

The Importance of Relaxation in Meditation

Relaxation is the first stage of meditation, the foundation of your Mental Resilience Training. Relaxation has physical and mental attributes, but physical stillness forms the basis of the relaxation process. In the context of meditation, relaxation provides real refreshment of the body and mind, which brings you to a state of equilibrium.

Many people begin a meditation practice but imagine they can skip the relaxation phase because it is not "the real meditation." However, if you don't achieve this stage of physical stillness, you will find yourself blocked from entering a deeper meditative state.

The Benefits of Relaxation

The most immediate benefit of practicing relaxation and meditation is learning to be still. Being still is an invigorating experience that gives you an immense sense of refreshment. The physiological benefits include decreased blood pressure, slower respiration and heart rate, reduced muscle tension, decreased stomach acid, lower blood cholesterol, and alpha and theta brain waves to enhance creative and cognitive processes.[3] Glimpses of mental clarity are a noticeable first sign that you have achieved a relaxed state.

Beginning to Relax

When you begin, use the audio to listen to the guided meditations. They resemble the training wheels on a bike; they're great for getting started, but after a while you may find that you no longer need them and can get to the relaxed state by yourself. This is up to you.

Some people find that they meditate regularly for a while but then lose the discipline and practice. If that happens and you would like to kick-start your practice again, then revisit the guided meditations. They are a great way to get back into the swing of things.

Mental Resilience Training Audio: Track 1 — Guided Relaxation

To begin the process of getting into a relaxed state, listen to track 1 of the audio. It provides a simple guided relaxation.

Both for beginners and more-experienced meditators, it is vital to cultivate physical stillness. This is a real skill that requires practice. Through physical stillness, you can achieve mental stillness.

Some may say that they already have a great deal of stillness in their lives, that in fact they are too still, even sedentary! They may well ask, "Aren't we supposed to be getting out and moving more?" The answer is complex; physical fitness is very important for achieving and maintaining health, but so is the right kind of stillness.

Do not underestimate the lack of physical stillness in your day-to-day life. Most people are unaware of just how much they move. It is unlikely that you can keep still for more than a few seconds on an average day. Even during sleep you toss and turn (have a look at the bedsheets after you wake up), so this may not be a completely restful experience. (For a deeper analysis of what happens to the body when it relaxes, refer to Herbert Benson's work *The Relaxation Response*.)

You can reach a relaxed state of mind by taking a structured approach such as the one that follows.

The Steps to Relaxation

STEP 1: If you wear glasses, take them off. Turn off your cell phone or pager, and if your PDA alarm is set, turn it off. Then lie down, as depicted in the illustration on the next page. As you relax, your body temperature drops, so you may want to cover yourself with a jacket or blanket. If you're at work and unable to lie down, do the next best thing: find an easy chair to relax in. Make sure that no matter what position you choose, your breathing is unconstrained and your abdomen can move freely in and out.

STEP 2: In this relaxation exercise, you will progressively bring your awareness to each part of the body. You will mentally scan each part of your body by focusing your attention precisely on

The Steps to Relaxation

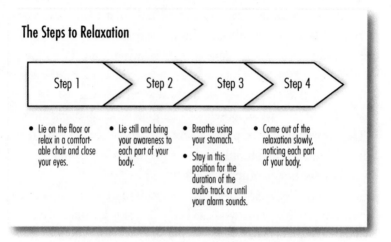

Step 1	Step 2	Step 3	Step 4
• Lie on the floor or relax in a comfortable chair and close your eyes.	• Lie still and bring your awareness to each part of your body.	• Breathe using your stomach. • Stay in this position for the duration of the audio track or until your alarm sounds.	• Come out of the relaxation slowly, noticing each part of your body.

that part, imagining your muscles softening and getting heavy. This allows excess energy to leave that part of the body, which is the beginning of the relaxation process. An effective way to scan the body is to feel the precise nature of the contact of the particular muscle or your skin with the floor or chair.

Bring your attention to each body part, in the sequence listed on the next page.

Relaxation Pose

1. Soles	14. Chest
2. Toes	15. Fingers
3. Ankles	16. Hands
4. Calves	17. Arms
5. Shins	18. Shoulders
6. Knees	19. Neck
7. Thighs	20. Forehead
8. Hips	21. Eyebrows
9. Buttocks	22. Eyes
10. Lower back	23. Cheeks
11. Middle back	24. Mouth
12. Upper back	25. Tongue
13. Stomach	

STEP 3: Focus on your breath, and notice your stomach rising and falling. If your attention wanders from your breath, gently bring it back. Whether you notice yourself becoming distracted by a noise outside the room or thinking about what you did before the relaxation, what you plan to do afterward, or what you want for lunch, just become more aware of the breath.

Frequently Asked Questions

How do I know if I am doing it right? When you find yourself worrying whether or not you're getting it right, remember, it's difficult to do it wrong! However, here are some pointers to making relaxation as effective as possible.

Understanding how the body responds to stressful situations may help you more easily get the picture. Relaxation activates your parasympathetic nervous system and deactivates your sympathetic nervous system. This slows down your heartbeat, lowers your blood pressure, increases blood flow to your internal organs, and generally decreases the hormone noradrenalin. So, as you wind down and destress, your metabolic rate decreases. As that happens during the relaxation exercise, your body starts to feel quite heavy. Some parts of your body may even start feeling a bit numb. You may feel cut off from your body, as if you are losing touch with your body and are only connected to your breath. You may also have a feeling of drifting or floating. Don't be alarmed; these are good responses.

What should I do to capture any amazing creative thoughts that arise during meditation? As you relax, you make space in your mind for thoughts. Many first-time meditators have wondrous, creative thoughts that bubble up as they begin to meditate. Many ask whether they should stop the meditation session and write down these thoughts, fearing that if they don't, the thoughts will be lost forever. Let me reassure you, these (and indeed, many other) thoughts will return after you finish your meditation, so you should not stop your session.

What happens if I fall asleep during meditation? Many people fall asleep in this part of the practice. It is okay! This is a natural response to the release of stress. If you fall asleep, it may mean that you need more sleep than you are currently getting. It may also indicate that your daily adrenalin or caffeine habit has kept you going artificially. You may notice that after waking from a nap during meditation, you feel very refreshed.

How do I move on to the next stage of meditation? There are no hard and fast rules, but generally when you can really relax for ten minutes without getting the urge to scratch or adjust yourself for four ·

sessions, then you know you are ready to go on to the next stage of meditation. If you pursue the twenty-one-day program presented at the end of this book, keep to the specified timetable.

Personal Encounters with Meditation

Sarah is a successful homemaker and career woman. She had given up full-time work to care for her two children, but even though she worked only three days a week, she ended up speaking to colleagues in her office most days.

"I am always on the move. Relaxation is the farthest thing from my mind. How do you relax when you have a two-year-old? As soon as he is down for his morning nap, I sit down and have a cup of coffee and start checking my emails. The caffeine hit allows me to keep going. Unfortunately it means that I can't get to sleep at night because I have so many things going through my mind. I end up feeling inadequate as a mom and a professional, which further adds to my stress. I started taking sleeping pills to knock me out, but that seemed only to numb me at nights and made me feel worse in the morning.

"Somebody mentioned that meditation would help me relax. I was reluctant at first. I knew it would take up precious time during my day, and I wasn't at all sure it would make me feel better. But I'm open to most things, so I tried it. I had very low expectations going in. I listened to the audio and found that the instructions helped me get the process.

"When I first started to relax I noticed all the pain I felt! First I felt the pain in my lower back. This was probably from picking up the kids continuously. Then I felt pain in my elbows and wrists. In a few minutes I felt as if my whole body were aching. The first few sessions I could not stop wriggling around. After a few sessions I tried to stay still and merely notice my discomfort rather than try to do anything about it. I noticed that the discomfort began to go away.

"I noticed that as I relaxed, my stomach started making gurgling noises. I felt a bit squeamish but it passed. Then thoughts started racing around my head, lists of things that I needed to do. But because I'd been warned this would happen, I kept coming back to the breath; I just kept with it. The bizarre thing is that for the first few sessions, I fell into a deep sleep. Only the gong at the end of the audio woke me up. It was so nice to drift off to sleep, and when I got up I felt a bit dreamy and gooey. I lay back down again and enjoyed the feeling of letting go. When I finally got up, I felt so refreshed.

"As I practiced more and more, my sleep patterns started getting better. I realized that if I relaxed during the day I would be able to sleep better. I was much more focused during the day and less irritable, and with the daily relaxation I stopped being in a half-awake, half-asleep state every day. It was wonderful!

"Now I try to meditate most days, but if I can't do a full meditation, I still never miss my ten to fifteen minutes of guided relaxation. I realize that I can do this anywhere. I have become really adept at achieving this deep state of relaxation. I have done it while waiting to pick up my kids from day care in the car. I have done it in the doctor's waiting room and in an airport lounge."

Many people are beginning to understand and use the benefits of a relaxation technique to help them become more effective in every part of their lives. Remember that relaxation is just the beginning. It can make a significant difference in the quality of your meditation practice.

Being physically still is the basis of the relaxation process. The relaxation technique presented in this chapter requires you to become consciously aware of each part of your body, allowing it to relax. Relaxation is the foundation of meditation.

CHAPTER EIGHT

becoming deeply calm

*Training began with children, who were taught
to sit still and enjoy it, to look where there was
apparently nothing to see, and to listen intently
when all seemingly was quiet.*

CHIEF SITTING BEAR

IN THE LAST CHAPTER, we considered the realm of relaxation and began to practice the techniques to achieve this physical awareness. While relaxation predominantly concerns our physical bodies, now it is time to look at the mental aspects of meditation, those that involve both body and mind.

Understanding Calm

Calm is a state of mind; it is also a stage in all meditations, including Mental Resilience Training. The calm stage involves your becoming aware of mental chatter, taking some steps to acknowledge it, and then reducing it using the skills and techniques you are learning.

What is the source and nature of all this mental chatter? It can be anything from a simple (but obsessive) thought to a complex story that keeps going around and around in your head. It could range from such thoughts as, "I really have put on weight!" or "I don't like that person" to "My relationship is getting more and more tense!" It could also involve more-productive thoughts such as, "I really need to plan for my next vacation" or "What present shall I get for my friend?"

This chatter can be detrimental to our sense of well-being. Too much chatter can exhaust us, and as the cycle continues we become more stressed. The more stressed we feel, the faster and louder the chatter seems to get.

The Importance of Meditative Calm

Calm is a state of being that allows you to perform at your peak. Often the only way to understand something is to consider its opposite. So, how does it feel when you are *not* calm? Have you ever come into work wondering how you were going to get through the day? Do you have days when there are so many things you need to do that not one of them gets accomplished properly? You start reading through important emails and then have to take a call. So you try to read the emails while on the phone, realizing that you are not doing either task very well. The caller senses that you are distracted, and you can't quite remember whether you replied to an email correctly. Because you switch back and forth between tasks, completing each only halfway, your struggle to maintain any focus starts to feel as if you've been merely spinning your wheels!

You know you have an important research report to read before a crucial meeting but realize that if you don't transfer some money into your checking account you might bounce the mortgage payment! You manage to go online and get your banking done, but then the phone rings again, and by the time you've put down the receiver your mind is even more scattered.

Now you have to attend a vital meeting at which you will be asked to make some crucial decisions. You sit down at the meeting, only to find that part of your mind is still at your desk. When we think many thoughts in quick succession or perform one activity after another, this is known as *dynamic thinking*. And dynamism is something to aspire to, right? Sure, it creates a tension that seems exciting, but ultimately it isn't truly productive. Consider the paradox, and sometimes the danger, that many people paid for high-level or creative decision making rarely have the appropriate creative time or creative "white space" in their work environments to achieve the clarity that's needed to make the best decisions.

Research has shown that we make our best decisions when we are calm.[1] The calmer you are, the more options you will probably consider; you will not only have a clearer immediate response but will more likely consider the second and third order of consequences of your actions and creatively think through a problem. We are at our most creative and innovative when in a calm state of mind.

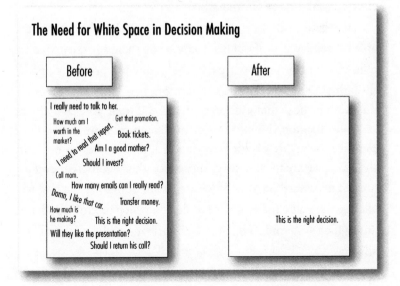

The Need for White Space in Decision Making

Before

I really need to talk to her.

How much am I worth in the market?

Get that promotion.

I need to read that report.

Book tickets.

Am I a good mother?

Should I invest?

Call mom.

How many emails can I really read?

Damn, I like that car.

Transfer money.

How much is he making?

This is the right decision.

Will they like the presentation?

Should I return his call?

After

This is the right decision.

The Benefits of Meditative Calm

When we are calm the information in our subconscious is far more accessible than when we are stressed. So, when calm we benefit from the ability to use more of our mental capacity than just our conscious mind. (See chapter 4, "A Model of the Mind.")

Developing meditative calm helps you in many parts of your life. It is certainly important in cultivating your meditation practice. It is also the tool that helps you remain focused in a heated debate or even an argument, and as stated above, it can be precisely what allows you to recognize the right course of action in a given moment.

Meditative calm is also about understanding where to place your energy. It helps you to develop focus, so that you no longer feel that your life is out of control or that you are merely spinning your wheels. You can start prioritizing your thoughts (and therefore your actions), choosing which to pursue and which to let go. Meditative calm will help you develop the mental muscles to concentrate and direct your thoughts.

Meditation allows you to change your thoughts. You become able to identify your thoughts, recognizing them as destructive or constructive. What you are and feel today are products of the thoughts you had yesterday. Therefore it is very important to be aware of how thoughts accumulate and their potential effect on you. To gain the most from this stage of your meditation practice, be aware of one very important idea: we are not our thoughts; we are the thinker of those thoughts, but those thoughts are not necessarily reality. If we are aware of this distinction, we can see the value in being able to decide which thoughts to have and which to avoid. This is a key part of building mental resilience.

Beginning to Develop Meditative Calm

This is the first practice you do sitting up. Once you have found a stable posture, start your practice. Initially your mind will keep on wandering. After some time, however, it will start to calm down. Remember, don't try to focus too hard. The most important thing is just to let go of the thoughts that come and go in your mind. Meditative calm will start to descend on you without any great effort.

Mental Resilience Training Audio: Track 2 — Meditative Calm

To begin the process of developing meditative calm and exercising your mental muscles, listen to track 2 of the audio. It provides a simple, guided meditation on meditative calm. I recommend practicing this breath meditation for a few weeks, observing yourself to see whether you're beginning to feel calmer day by day. The twenty-one-day program outlined in chapter 12 advises practicing this technique every day after the fifth day.

In the guided meditation you will hear how to use your breath to achieve meditative calm. The meditation asks you to focus on breathing, placing all your attention on the in and out breaths.

You may find it useful to count your breaths (say, from one to five) and then repeat the sequence. You will invariably notice thoughts entering your mind. Do not be alarmed or disrupted by them. Know that they are just thoughts. Acknowledge the thoughts by giving each one a generic label such as *work; husband, wife, kids, boyfriend, girlfriend; money*, or *worry*. As you label each thought, do not linger on it, but return your focus to your breath.

Be in awe of your breath. It may sound strange, but because it is so automatic we tend to take breathing completely for granted! In this meditation we are becoming aware of the power, magic, and beauty of the simple act of breathing. To get the maximum benefit, regard your breath with awe. Breathing is the process that keeps us alive, day in and day out. The breath does not rest for even a few minutes, and we need to pay respect to this amazing bodily function.

If your mind wanders from your breath, perhaps imagining being unable to breathe will help you concentrate on it a bit more easily. Imagine that you are at the beach, a wave has just knocked you underwater, and you are struggling to get up. You are on your last breath, but just before getting your lungs full of water, you come up and burst above the water into the fresh air. Imagine the feeling as you take that first breath: "Aah! Wow, what an amazing breath!" You can feel the life returning to your lungs. Sense the thrill of it. This is the kind of awe I would like you to have when you practice breath awareness meditation.

Is there anything more satisfying, more healing, more enjoyable,
more important in your life than your next breath?
Don't let it go by unnoticed. Take your time and savor it.

BETH JOHNSON

The Steps to Meditative Calm

STEP 1: Assume a comfortable posture before beginning meditation. Scan your body to bring awareness to each part.

STEP 2: Become aware of your breathing. Bring your awareness to your out breath. Particularly notice the sensation of friction from the air passing by the tip of your nose as you breathe out. The mere act of focusing on your out breath will help you become calm. If you would like, you can choose to count your out breaths. Try saying silently to yourself, "One out, two out, three out, four out, five out." Once you have counted to five, start the sequence again from one.

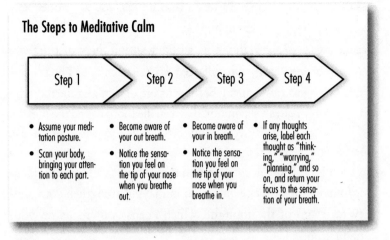

The Steps to Meditative Calm

Step 1	Step 2	Step 3	Step 4
• Assume your meditation posture. • Scan your body, bringing your attention to each part.	• Become aware of your out breath. • Notice the sensation you feel on the tip of your nose when you breathe out.	• Become aware of your in breath. • Notice the sensation you feel on the tip of your nose when you breathe in.	• If any thoughts arise, label each thought as "thinking," "worrying," "planning," and so on, and return your focus to the sensation of your breath.

STEP 3: Bring your awareness to your in breath. Particularly notice the sensation of friction from the air passing by the tip of your nose. You may notice that your in breath feels a little cooler than your out breath.

Focusing on your in breath will help you become more alert to the mental chatter. If you would like, you can choose to count your in breaths. Try saying silently to yourself, "One in, two in, three in, four in, five in." Once you have reached five, restart the sequence from one.

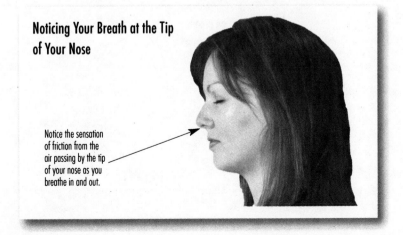

Noticing Your Breath at the Tip of Your Nose

Notice the sensation of friction from the air passing by the tip of your nose as you breathe in and out.

STEP 4: As you begin to focus on your breath, you will notice how various thoughts come in and out of your consciousness. To become aware of these thoughts without letting them distract you from your breathing, you will need to label each one. The process of labeling ensures that you become aware of thinking the thought; it therefore creates a separation between the thought and the thinker.

The more clarity you bring to this labeling, the easier it will be for you to have a thought, identify or label it, and let it go. By refraining from concentrating on the content while merely identifying the thought as a particular kind, you strengthen your ability to let go of the thought, which keeps your focus on your meditation.

Each time a thought distracts you from awareness of your breath, slowly bring your attention back. This mental wandering will happen many times. Just as we need to repeatedly lift weights in the gym to build up our physical muscles, we also repeatedly have to bring our awareness back to our breath to develop our mental muscles.

What Happens during Meditation

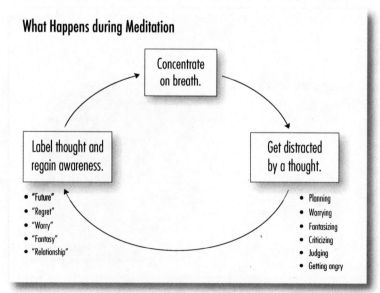

Frequently Asked Questions

How do I know if I am doing it right? This question comes up a lot. Remember the metaphor of the glass of dirty water. Though there seemed to be a great deal of mud in the solution, the mere act of becoming still allowed the dirt to settle and the water to get clearer and clearer. That's all you have to do in this meditation: keep still and notice the breath.

If your awareness of your breath has increased, you are doing it right! Avoid the expectation that something monumental is supposed occur while you are sitting, and you will be fine. All it takes is a bit of time.

I am starting to experience different sensations in my body. What does this mean? As you become calmer, you will have some unusual sensations. You may experience some of the following:

Heaviness — You may begin to feel as if your body is weighed down, that you are aware of the weight of the various parts of your body and that they feel heavy. You may lose the awareness of where parts of your body begin or end; for example, you might know where the perimeters of your arms are without being able to tell how they relate to your shoulders or hands; perhaps everything feels like a solid mass.

Lightness — You may feel that your body is particularly light, or you may be unable to feel your body; for example, you know that your body parts are present, but they feel very light, as if levitating from the surface you're sitting on. Some people describe a sensation of being out of their bodies, and while you may feel this, you are (unfortunately) not physically levitating.

Tingling and warmth — Another indication of calm is a sense of tingling or warmth on the skin. Your skin feels as though it's coming alive, which may be pleasant or somewhat disturbing. You are actually experiencing an increased awareness of ordinary sensations. Because your mind is calm, with reduced mental clutter, you become aware of various sensations that you normally don't notice. The good thing is, they will mostly feel exquisite!

Aches and pains — Do not be alarmed if you start to notice an increase in minor aches and pains. You may think, "These aches and pains are arising because I'm meditating," but that's not really the case. Actually the mind is becoming free of clutter so that you start noticing the aches and pains that are usually present day to day. You come to realize how tense various parts of your body are and, most important, become able to relax and let go of some of that everyday tension.

Changes in breathing — The other thing you might notice is a change in your breathing. Your breath will become very fine and soft. In India, yogis measure their mental calm by how far away from their noses they can feel the breath. The more agitated you are, the farther away your breath will feel from your nose. The calmer you are, the closer your breath gets. The subtler the breath, the calmer the mind. Some students notice that the breath has become so subtle it feels as if they are not breathing at all! Don't worry. You will not stop breathing during meditation.

Why do we use our breath as the focus of meditation? We use our breath as a calming tool because the body responds very positively to breathing! Whenever you feel stressed and want to calm down, you will (consciously or unconsciously) take a deep breath. Why is that? The breath is the link between the mind and body. The rate and depth of your breath indicate how agitated or calm you are. The breath is one of nature's most reliable and obvious biofeedback mechanisms. Just notice the next time you or somebody else is angry; the breath is strong and quite audible. Also notice when you are calm; for example, when listening to a beautiful piece of music or working on something you enjoy. Your breath is very subtle and even.

When we are stressed our breathing becomes shallow. Shallow breathing is when we take only a small amount of breath into our lungs, usually by drawing air into the chest area using the smaller intercostal muscles rather than the stronger diaphragm. In severe cases shallow breathing can result in hyperventilation. Often we unconsciously breathe shallowly throughout the day.

The problem with shallow breathing is that it does not provide enough oxygen to our brains and cells. Insufficient oxygen in the tissues, or hypoxia, has been linked with degenerative disease. Shallow, short, and fast breathing can increase stress, asthma, fatigue, insomnia, and many other ailments. Doctors William J. Elliot and Joseph L. Izzo, both of whom are professors of medicine at Rush Medical College in Chicago, found a major favorable impact from deep breathing on high blood pressure, which is a major contributing factor to heart attack.[2]

Remember, the breath is always there and it is universal. There are no religious connotations to the breath. Whether you are an atheist, Hindu, Muslim, Christian, Jew, Sikh, or Buddhist you have breath. Breath is sacred because it keeps you alive; you do not need to have any faith in its potency.

We can always use our breath as a tool. We don't have to light a candle or take a set of beads with us wherever we go, because breathing is always with us. If you want to practice breath awareness meditation in a taxi or while waiting in line at the supermarket, you can do it. Some of my students use this form of meditation while driving in heavy traffic — with their eyes open, I must add!

Breath is the most precious thing in our lives and, obviously, something we can't survive without. We can live without water for approximately two to three days, and without food for even longer. But we cannot live without breathing for more than just a few minutes. Noticing our breath brings our minds back to the present moment, the place where there is no future and no past.

So your breath gives you instant and powerful feedback to your mental state. Have you ever noticed that when you're about to call somebody you'd rather not speak to, you instinctively breathe in deeply and sigh? Your mind automatically switches to autopilot to alert you that a stressful situation is coming up.

The next time you are agitated, become aware of your breath. Once you do that, it is very difficult to stay agitated; you have to come back to the present.

Breath is the most precious thing we have, but we cannot hold onto it. Therefore it can provide us with a great lesson on the value of being in the present moment.

Breath is the link between our conscious and subconscious minds. It is remarkable because it works whether or not we are conscious of it, for example, during sleep. Our breath is one of the main keys to opening up the gateways between our conscious and subconscious minds.

What do I do about this song going over and over in my mind? When you start sitting to meditate, things that have been stored up in your subconscious emerge into your conscious mind. All you need to do is be aware of the thought, song, or issue, and after a while it will stop. Beginning meditators hear advertising jingles or verses from familiar songs when they first practice, but these distractions soon diminish and then disappear.

What's a mantra, and why don't we use it as a meditation object? Many people exploring meditation have heard the term *mantra*. A mantra is a word, chant, or sound that is repeated over and over in the meditation process to reduce mental agitation. The repetition helps calm the mind, but there is also the risk that it will numb the mind. The very act of repetition potentially reduces agitation but doesn't develop insights as to its cause. Thus while you may achieve some calm, you don't necessarily clear the real source of the agitation. In the process of Mental Resilience Training, you will find the tools to investigate and release the agitation, not merely suppress it.

Personal Encounters with Meditation

Jake is a futures broker who characterizes himself as a work hard, play hard guy. When Jake wants to relax, he drinks beer or watches sports. But in time neither activity helps him relax. He begins to feel that he can't switch off and struggles to sleep at nights, which starts to depress him so that he ends up more stressed. He tries taking antidepressants but they don't help his sleep.

Jake's girlfriend is concerned and asks him to go to a meditation session. Jake's not really interested but goes along to humor her. In the first relaxation session he goes into a deep sleep. This surprises him because lately he hasn't been able to easily fall asleep. Immediately after the session he buys a CD of guided meditations. After one week of meditating, his sleep patterns improve, and though he doesn't sleep more than four or five hours a night, this is better than before.

"In the beginning of the session, I was lying there trying to take it all in. I felt as if I could not fill my lungs with enough air. I just wanted to keep on breathing. My whole body felt numb, as if I were melting into the floor. I felt as if I were looking down at my body. My mind fought the sensation for a while, but then it just gave up and let go.

"The sleep I had after my meditation session was really deep. I realized that I had forgotten how to switch off. This technique was so basic but really effective in lowering my mental activity. It was strange to realize that I actually had to work at switching off.

"I really enjoyed using the breath as a meditation object, because when I arrived I was determined that, if asked to chant something, I would simply walk out of the building. I really was not into this New Age mumbo jumbo. I would've been happy to get a good night's sleep, but there was no way I was going to get in touch with the energy of crystals, which is how I imagined the meditation teachers would speak about this.

"I found meditation hard at first. I realized I was trying too hard. I'm a competitive person, and I really thought I had to nail this. I was even competing with my girlfriend to see if I could be better at this than she was. When I started letting go of trying to be good at it, I started to get what it was all about.

"It is now an important part of my life. I am not sure how good a meditator I am, but who cares? I feel better and sleep better. At work, when I feel stressed I think of the sensations I feel during meditation, and I instantly start taking deeper breaths. I feel much less irritable. I have a lot more focus at work, I think because I have developed my powers of concentration."

Developing meditative calm is important in your meditation practice because it is part of the overall skill set you are learning. Calm is the tool that helps you recognize the right course of action for yourself, allowing you to respond to any situation with an effective decision.

Meditative calm helps reduce mental chatter, and calm results when we focus on our breath. Labeling our thoughts helps us become aware of, and slowly let go of, them so we can find a calm place within ourselves.

Meditative calm helps you develop focus, so that, instead of feeling as if your life is out of control, you can start prioritizing your thoughts. Calm helps us focus and develop mental muscles, which is the first stage in developing mental resilience.

CHAPTER NINE

developing emotional tranquility

Your vision will become clear only when you can look into your heart. Who looks outside, dreams. Who looks inside, awakes.

CARL JUNG

IN THE PREVIOUS CHAPTER we learned how to develop calm, predominantly in our conscious minds. In this chapter we will discover how to develop a sense of tranquility in both the conscious and subconscious minds.

Understanding Emotional Tranquility

Emotional tranquility is a state of being that happens when we feel positive, peaceful emotions within us and toward those around us. These emotions make us feel mentally resilient. When we experience this state, we can cope much better with whatever life offers us, as well as better support others.

As with many concepts, particularly those related to emotional versus centered states, it is easier to understand what each is when we think about its opposite. So let's first imagine how the absence of emotional tranquility might feel.

Most of us have had an argument with a loved one from time to time. Did the argument fill your thoughts for hours afterward? Did you think about it in the shower before work or during the drive to the office? After you arrived at work and tried to focus on a task, perhaps your mind continued replaying the argument. Naturally, under such circumstances focusing on your work would be extremely difficult. As you become more skilled at meditation you will drop such thoughts at will during meditation practice and become able to drop them at will in your day-to-day life.

Another example most of us can relate to is receiving an apparently rude email to which we respond by banging out an equally terse one and prematurely hitting the send button. Later, when we have calmed down and reread the email, we suspect we may have overreacted. Such a spontaneous response would probably have some unfortunate consequences.

In these situations we may find ourselves experiencing a range of difficult emotions, some so intense that we may even feel as if we are falling apart. Often we have to keep performing at work while struggling to handle difficult emotions swirling inside us. We may even start feeling depressed (I have heard this from many of my students who have undergone difficult divorces and breakups). By continually indulging such thoughts, we become mentally exhausted. If we allow this emotional exhaustion to occur for too long, it can become depression.

Even though you may be highly skilled in your job, if you're in a poor emotional state, your performance invariably deteriorates. (Just consider whether you'd like a surgeon operating on you immediately after she discovered her partner was having an affair! You'd decline, no matter how fantastic her track record.)

The Importance of Emotional Tranquility

Emotions drive every part of our lives. Many emotions are submerged in the subconscious mind, so we're unaware of them, and yet they are very powerful. We like to think that we remain very rational in our decision making, keeping emotions out of the equation. But whether we are choosing a partner, making an investment, or buying a car, we may take in all the data, do the analysis, and, even then, make the final decision based on how things feel! For example, when choosing a partner, you might be drawn to a person with certain traits that you're not really aware of; you don't really understand why you find this person attractive. Usually, that potential partner sets off emotions or connects to something deep within your subconscious, compelling you to respond.

> *Let's not forget that the little emotions are the great captains
> of our lives, and we obey them without realizing it.*
>
> VINCENT VAN GOGH

Even the most numerically oriented people are guided by emotions in most analytical situations. Many people pride themselves on their objectivity in decision making, imagining that they use solely facts and figures to assess a situation. But as I learned in the investment markets, "money always follows a good story." Analysts can investigate the numbers all they want, but investors and investment professionals invariably are persuaded as much by a good story as by impeccable numbers. If there is an emotional component and the investors relate to it, that's the story they go with.

The Infectiousness of Emotional States

Just as a lack of emotional tranquility can be transferred to people around us, so can its opposite. Emotional tranquility is not just important for our well-being; it also affects the people around us. David Busch, a Vietnam veteran, recounted an extreme and powerful example of this characteristic.

Very early in the Vietnam War, an American platoon was hunkered down in the heat of a firefight with the Vietcong. Suddenly, in the midst of the bullets a line of six monks began walking along the elevated berms that separated the rice paddies. Perfectly calm and poised, the monks walked directly toward the line of fire.

"They didn't look right; they didn't look left. They walked straight through," recalls David, who was in the American platoon. "It was really strange, because nobody shot at 'em. And after they walked over the berms, suddenly all the fight was out of me. I just didn't feel like I wanted to do this anymore, at least not that day. It must have been that way for everybody, because everybody quit. We stopped fighting."[1]

The power of the monks' courageous calm to pacify soldiers in the heat of battle illustrates a basic principle: emotions are contagious.

The Power of Choice

There are various ways to develop awareness or sensitivity in our conscious and subconscious minds. Awareness allows us to make the right choices, not necessarily to change what happens to us but to change how we respond to what happens.

Unfortunately many people have been victimized or treated badly in the past, possibly from bullying at school, sibling rivalry, or even harsh words from a parent. The incident may have been minor; however, the effects can remain with us for a long time. For some people it is extreme, for example, a Buddhist monk facing daily repression by the authorities in Tibet or a concentration camp inmate facing daily torture by the Nazis.

In such extreme situations the victims might be justified in harboring deep resentment, fury, or even a need for revenge. Such feelings or desires are likely to remain part of the victims' emotional makeup forever. However, even in such extreme circumstances we still have the ability to respond in a different way.

Viktor Frankl is professor of neurology and psychiatry at University of Vienna Medical School. During World War II he spent three years in Auschwitz, Dachau, and other concentration camps. He wrote *Man's Search for Meaning*, a testimony to the power of choice in healing. Frankl recalls:

"We who lived in concentration camps can remember the men who walked through the huts comforting others, giving away their last piece of bread. They may have been few in number, but they offer sufficient proof that everything can be taken from a man but one thing: the last of the human freedoms — to choose one's attitude in any given set of circumstances, to choose one's own way."[2]

Another example comes in the form of an anecdote from a collection of conversations with the Dalai Lama. The Dalai Lama met a fellow monk who had spent eighteen years in a Chinese prison. Seeing that the monk had remained unchanged despite many years of hardship, the Dalai Lama asked, "Wasn't there a time when you were afraid?" The monk replied, "I was most afraid that I might come to hate the Chinese, that I might lose my sense of mercy."[3]

We have many emotional responses to the world around us. Sometimes they dissipate, and other times they remain within us. Negative emotional states can be present in our subconscious and unconscious minds for a long time. Have you noticed how some people mention hurts they experienced years before, recalling and

feeling them as if they happened in the immediate past? The negative emotions are still present, but now they are in the subconscious mind, which can potentially affect everything a person sees,
feels, hears, touches, or experiences.

Note that every emotion has a purpose; even anger, depression, and grief serve a purpose in our lives. The negativity arises
when we try to suppress these emotions rather than accept them,
thereby letting them go. When an emotion stops serving our well-
being we need to develop an understanding of how to drop it.

The emotional distress of long-held hurts causes exhaustion.
It can contribute to feelings of depression, agitation, and anger. It
is like a virus on your hard drive (the subconscious mind), which
every now and then causes your computer to break down.

Begin to observe what sets you off. As you become more
aware, you can better control your reactions. I like to think of
some of the emotions buried in our subconscious as land mines.
They are hard to spot, but if you go anywhere near them, they
explode. Has someone's seemingly innocuous remark ever just
set you off? Perhaps when reflecting on the incident you think, "I
shouldn't have responded so aggressively or forcefully." That
remark may have inadvertently triggered something very deep
inside you, maybe something from your childhood, such as a
deprecating remark from your elementary-school teacher or a
parental rebuke. However, in the heat of the moment it is very
difficult to know what you are really responding to.

Understanding our emotional makeup means finding those
hidden land mines that are buried in our subconscious. As we will
see, these potential bombs may also be treasure chests!

Acting Rather Than Reacting

In the face of unpleasant feelings, you may feel as if you have no
control, but if you maintain awareness you can take action from a

sense of calm. You can choose to experience the unpleasant feeling, and by noticing how it makes you feel, you can then decide how you prefer to respond, from the range of available responses.

This ability to take control requires energy and, most important, awareness. In any situation it is crucial to remember that you don't have to react spontaneously. Instead it is very important to learn to be aware of your feelings. Tranquility meditation actively uses our emotions to generate pleasant and unpleasant feelings inside us, both of which we observe. The tranquility meditation allows you to be comfortable with your entire range of feelings. As you become aware of your unpleasant feelings and start to become comfortable with them, you will begin to make informed choices rather than react from hidden or obvious emotional states.

One of the skills we gain during Mental Resilience Training is being comfortable with discomfort, which allows us to make decisions driven by our value systems, rather than an aversion to discomfort or a craving for comfort. One vital thing to bear in mind is that unpleasant feelings are not necessarily negative.

On the flip side, not everything that feels pleasant in the moment is necessarily positive! For example, you may indulge a craving for fattening fast food and feel good about it for a while, but later you might have regrets, and your indulgence may hurt you in the long term. Everybody has spontaneously responded to an incident and later regretted it. Perhaps you've looked back and thought, "I really wish I hadn't screamed at that driver or insulted that store clerk." Being sensitive to your emotional state and able to take the heat out of difficult emotions can help prevent such regrets.

This mental capacity, mental resilience, is what you will hone with the emotional tranquility meditation. You will find a growing sense of endurance, which will help you begin to overcome the emotional exhaustion that takes place when dealing with distressful emotions.

The Mother Teresa Effect

My teacher Nanda used to list the benefits of emotional tranquility meditation and the power of love as a meditation topic. One of the physiological benefits he mentioned was that if you were sick with a sore throat or cold, and meditated, you would recover faster. I used to humor him by saying that I believed all the benefits. But really this was a bit too much for my cynical teenage mind.

I might have continued to ignore his belief in the physiological effects had I not come across some research a few years ago that discussed the "Mother Teresa effect." Mother Teresa was a Nobel Peace Prize laureate who dedicated her life to the poor of Calcutta, India. Psychologist David McClelland spent several months studying the responses of Harvard students to a documentary showing Mother Teresa in Calcutta working compassionately among India's poor. McClelland documented a sharp increase in the Immunoglobulin-A (IgA) content in the saliva of the students immediately after they viewed the film. Why did this matter? Well, IgA, which is created by our immune system, is the first line of defense against infection (particularly colds and flu), and works by attacking viral infections.[4]

Later work documenting this effect had the students spend an hour thinking deeply about two subjects: a time in their lives when they felt loved and cared for by someone, and a time when they loved someone. The effects on their immune systems replicated those of the first experiment, in which they had viewed the Mother Teresa documentary. The simple act of imagining the love in their own lives had strengthened the immune response of all participants.

Beginning to Develop Emotional Tranquility

This is the third stage in your practice. Having developed a bit of calm in the previous stage, you can now progress to emotional tranquility. To create emotional tranquility we use strong emotions such as love and compassion. As you become more adept at creating these emotions inside you, your level of emotional tranquility will increase naturally.

Mental Resilience Training Audio: Track 3 — Emotional Tranquility

To begin the process of achieving emotional tranquility, listen to track 3 of the audio accompanying this book. It provides a simple guided meditation that will deepen the practice you have already begun. This stage of meditation helps you develop sustained concentration, an extremely useful tool that will help you monitor the destructive emotions whirling inside without letting them distract or distress you.

In the tranquility stage of Mental Resilience Training, we are developing an awareness of our emotional states and, whenever possible, encouraging constructive emotions. As we practice this meditation, we focus on what happens inside ourselves during various emotional experiences.

Remember that the emotional balance this meditation cultivates is contagious. People around you will start sharing your emotional tranquility.

Types of Thoughts to Notice

What is your opinion of yourself? Are you quietly satisfied, or even happy, with the kind of person you are, or are you dissatisfied with aspects of yourself?

Many of us are insecure overachievers working really hard to overcome an innate sense of self-dissatisfaction. People constantly push themselves, out of a need to prove that they are worthy and significant. Many workaholics seem to crave some sense of acceptance, perhaps first from themselves, and then others. Because they desperately need to prove their worth, their work and personal lives become grossly imbalanced.

Self-acceptance is even more crucial in relationships. It's very difficult to be in a relationship and to allow someone to love you if you don't accept yourself. If you're looking for another person to provide the love you lack within yourself, your relationship could face difficulties.

Most people are their own harshest critics, so learning about self-love is critical. Most of us need to show more kindness to ourselves.

Have you ever had a performance appraisal from a boss or a report card from a teacher that mentioned five strong, positive traits but ended with one small criticism? What was your response? What was your mind's response? For most people, the mind automatically dwells on that last criticism. This all-too-common response forms much of the mental chatter we experience during meditation.

This meditation will also reveal how much we continually judge others, from our in-laws to our colleagues, from the slow driver on the freeway to the cranky shop assistant. This constant judging is another primary source of mental chatter, and to decrease it while increasing emotional tranquility, we need to change our thoughts, which starts with wishing everyone around us happiness or calm. This may feel false at first, but the intentional act of blessing others eventually changes our thought patterns. As we become kinder to ourselves and the people around us, the disruptive and destructive mental chatter decreases.

To achieve emotional tranquility practice the following:

- Think of the things you like about yourself (make a mental list of your good points), and then notice how that feels within your body.
- Think of someone you love, and experience how that makes you feel.
- Think of an acquaintance about whom you have no strong feelings, positive or negative, and generate compassion and kindness toward that person, noticing what you feel in your body.
- Think of someone with whom you are experiencing conflict, and notice what happens in your body when you wish that person well.

The Steps to Emotional Tranquility

STEP 1: Show kindness to yourself. The first step in emotional tranquility meditation is to focus on yourself by developing love or acceptance and showing kindness to yourself. These days, showing kindness to ourselves might seem somewhat narcissistic. However, this meditation is not about building up our ego but rather about accepting ourselves for exactly who we are right now.

First starting the emotional tranquility meditation can feel uncomfortable. What's important is to take time to listen to all the feelings and emotions that emerge. Think about your own acts of kindness. Recall those instances when you went out of your way to help someone or did something to make someone's life better. Remember the times when you put others' needs before your own.

Alternatively, think about how others might describe you. Imagine the nice things they might say and notice which ones you really relate to. Rather than obviously flattering statements that

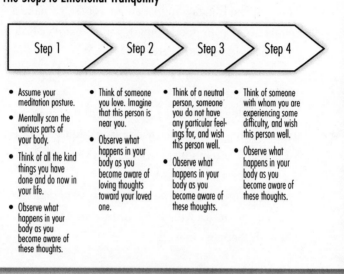

The Steps to Emotional Tranquility

Step 1 > **Step 2** > **Step 3** > **Step 4**

Step 1
- Assume your meditation posture.
- Mentally scan the various parts of your body.
- Think of all the kind things you have done and do now in your life.
- Observe what happens in your body as you become aware of these thoughts.

Step 2
- Think of someone you love. Imagine that this person is near you.
- Observe what happens in your body as you become aware of loving thoughts toward your loved one.

Step 3
- Think of a neutral person, someone you do not have any particular feelings for, and wish this person well.
- Observe what happens in your body as you become aware of these thoughts.

Step 4
- Think of someone with whom you are experiencing some difficulty, and wish this person well.
- Observe what happens in your body as you become aware of these thoughts.

are easily dismissed, try to recall positive feedback you've received about the way you positively impacted someone's life. Keep returning to your own feelings about what others say, and what sensations they bring about for you.

If you find this step difficult, try to visualize giving yourself a hug or a pat on the back, or just wishing yourself happiness. You can wish yourself more peace of mind or freedom from worry about your career, loved ones, or health. Note that this differs greatly from practicing affirmations; this is not about affirming how wonderful you are or that you are becoming a better person or growing day by day. You may be all of those things, but your aim here is to create inner feelings of caring, tenderness, and kindness toward yourself. Especially when they begin, a lot of people leave out this section because they don't feel anything for themselves. If that is the case for you, go on to step 2 after you have attempted step 1, but don't get bogged down. Then, next time you practice the emotional tranquility meditation, come back to step 1 and see if it feels any different.

To love oneself is the beginning of a lifelong romance.

OSCAR WILDE

STEP 2: Show kindness to someone you love. The second part of the emotional tranquility meditation involves focusing on a loved one, perhaps your partner or a friend. It can be your parents, children, or grandparents, anybody you have a lot of affection for. Try not to think of someone who sexually arouses you, because what you want to feel is love, not lust! You are after a warm, fuzzy feeling inside, not one that gets your pulse racing.

Think about the person and notice how you feel. Notice the sensations that arise in your body when you wish that person happiness and protection. Many of my students report a tingling in the stomach or warmness in the chest. Such responses vary from session to session depending on the person in mind.

STEP 3: Show kindness to someone you feel neutral about. The next step in the meditation is to focus on a person whom you know but don't have a particularly strong feeling about, someone who is neutral. This person can be someone whom you've just met but don't know very well. Whenever you think about that person, you may simply get a blank feeling. I find it useful to concentrate on someone who has just walked past and said hello, or a person reported about in the news who is having hard times. The person can be young or old; it does not matter. Once again, try not to focus on someone you find physically attractive. If you find it hard to think of being kind to someone you don't know, remember the compassion that many people showed to victims of some recent natural disaster. Even though the victims are strangers to us, seeing parents who have lost their children or children who have lost their families creates very powerful emotions within us. In this type of situation such a huge outpouring of compassion and help goes to people most of us do not know and will never know.

When you think about the neutral person you've selected for this step, wish that person all the very best. Avoid the blank "have a nice day" of a checkout clerk or bank teller. It doesn't sound convincing and may not be sincere. This part of the meditation requires that you really mean it when you say it, that you truly wish that person a wonderful life.

STEP 4: Show kindness to a difficult person. Next, focus on someone with whom you are experiencing difficulty. Wish that person well; wish them happiness and health. Be conscious of what happens in your body, and notice the physical sensations that arise when you think about this person.

During this meditation, you don't have to focus on just one person. You can switch among different people. Try to select someone who will not make you so upset that you won't be able to keep sitting in meditation. Initially try to find someone who upsets you only a little. Then, as your mind becomes stronger, focus on a person who upsets you a lot. However, do not turn your meditation session into a trial of will. It should be enjoyable.

Obviously this meditation can have useful effects in your daily life. You may find that your interactions with the person gradually improve, or notice that now you can interact with him or her without tightening up or getting as anxious as before. You may notice this person responding to you more favorably and that your relationship has improved. Also if you keep this person in your awareness during multiple meditation sessions, you may not be as defensive or aggressive when you engage with him or her, which may allow for a constructive discussion the next time you meet.

Frequently Asked Questions

When I practice this meditation, nothing seems to happen; no emotions or feelings seem to arise. What should I do? Some of my students comment that they do not experience any emotions when they begin this stage of the meditation. This frequently happens with my male students, who may have been discouraged from expressing their emotions as children. In response, the students speed up the technique, hoping to speed up the process. However, the main emphasis of this technique is to observe your body, to observe the sensations that occur when you bring certain people to mind. The more slowly you practice the emotional tranquility meditation, the more powerful it is and the more emotional tranquility you will develop.

Imagine driving down a dirt road through a forest. You are going reasonably fast, taking in the scenery; the trees move by quite fast, and the road is a brown blur. Sure, you are having a forest experience, but are you truly experiencing the forest?

Now imagine yourself walking in the forest. Perhaps you see an occasional bird or other animal. You may notice the color of the trees much more clearly than you would if you were driving. Now what would happen if you actually stopped and sat down in the forest, and became aware of what was happening around you? You might become aware of insects and the unique sounds they make. Perhaps you would notice the colors and shapes of the leaves of various trees; you might be lucky enough to see an animal stroll close by.

You can equally apply this process of slowing down and observing to your emotions. Initially your emotions are quite difficult to engage. If you rush the emotional tranquility meditation, you won't experience much. But as you practice, your emotions, like the wildlife in the forest, will emerge very slowly and tentatively. All you need to do is observe. The more you slow down and observe, the more aware of your emotional wildlife you will be. As emotions emerge, they will become more apparent to you in your daily life. You can act from emotional awareness, thereby making better decisions. You will overcome experiencing unpredictable actions and mental states.

So I encourage you not to speed through this part of the meditation technique. Again, this technique differs from the affirmations you may have heard or read about. You may not start feeling better right away. This is not a quick-fix approach to feeling good about yourself. (However, be warned; it does have this side effect!)

Our focus is becoming aware of the emotions inside us and noticing what we feel in our bodies when these emotions arise. It is important to develop this emotional intelligence, so we can choose to experience a deep level of tranquility.

Why do we use love to gain emotional tranquility? We know that love is a very powerful emotion, so we use this emotion to understand our emotional landscape. It's a fact that one of the reasons for the popularity of chocolate is that eating it provides the same chemicals to your brain (namely, phenylethylamine, anandamine, and tryptophan) as those released when you're in love. This is probably why many people are addicted to it! Also if you show more love to yourself, the receptors in your cells become more receptive to love chemicals produced in your thyroid, so you begin to feel better. The need to love and be loved is a driving force in our lives. And most would agree that during periods when we experience significant love in our lives, we feel demonstrably better. This meditation technique seeks to develop increased emotional contentment or feelings of love within your mind and heart.

However, I should warn you that people who feel more love become much more lovable! You've probably noticed this around colleagues or friends who are in love. Sure, they may seem starry-eyed every now and then, but there's a contagious sense of energy and purpose in their lives. Essentially the loving-kindness you feel toward yourself and others will certainly affect the stories you tell yourself. The mental chatter will diminish as you start feeling good about yourself. More important, you will actually stop hurting yourself with destructive stories.

This sense of well-being also makes you less judgmental. You stop viewing other people critically, and over time you start seeing others as having very similar needs to your own.

Are we trying to bliss out and forget our responsibilities? Emotional tranquility meditation is not about blissing out. It is an exploration of yourself and your emotional makeup. You are exploring your submerged emotions through one of the most powerful emotions that we all have — love.

Becoming aware of your emotional makeup will allow you to stay healthier both physically and mentally. The connection between emotions and chemical interactions in our bodies is becoming more documented as clinical research extends into this area. In *Molecules of Emotion* Candace Pert describes the research on the way chemicals inside our bodies form a dynamic information network, linking mind and body. Awareness of this link, through emotional awareness, is critical to our mental and physical well-being.

You mention emotions and feelings as if they are different things. I thought they were the same. When you practice the emotional tranquility meditation it is important to understand the difference between feelings and emotions. We use words such as *feelings* and *emotions* interchangeably, but it's important to draw a distinction. I have found it useful in my own teaching and practice to distinguish between the two.

Feelings refers to our basic gut-level likes and dislikes, and there are three kinds: pleasant, unpleasant, and neutral. When you hug your loved one, you probably feel pleasant feelings. Unpleasant feelings might arise when you go to the dentist for a painful procedure, and neutral feelings come from routine activities that evoke neither happiness nor sadness, such as combing your hair.

Your responses to your feelings are automatic; it is very hard to control them. For example, if you touch a hot kettle, you will automatically pull your hand away and yelp, "Ow!" Your body's response to the burn is automatic. However, the emotions you have about that burn are in your control. You can either accept the incident or let it ruin your day. It is very hard to control whether we like or dislike something at any given moment. Also our likes and dislikes change over time. For example, as a kid you may have felt very upset when your mom plunked down a lot of vegetables on your plate. As you grew older and became more attuned to eating vegetables as a healthy lifestyle choice, you may have begun seeking out and enjoying meals with lots of vegetables. As an adult, you learn to master your emotions around vegetables.

Emotions refers to the active responses that arise from your feelings. So, based on an unpleasant feeling, you might have an emotional response of aggression or ill will. When you are not aware of them, these emotional responses arise automatically and very quickly. However, when you are aware, you actually have more choices about how to respond. You can respond with more emotional intelligence than from a pure emotional reaction.

A student offered me the following example: She had to attend a board meeting whose agenda included some discussion of very personal issues. After many years of meditation and awareness of her feelings, she was aware of her feelings as she entered the meeting. When difficult issues were brought up, she became aware of tightness in her chest, heaviness in her stomach, and shortness of breath. Instead of going into her fight-or-flight response, which, in this case, would've been fight, she took one step back and became aware of the unpleasant feelings inside her. She was then able to consciously decide how to react rather than merely react unthinkingly. So her emotional response was to slow down her natural tendency to react, then respond to the board's concerns rather than personally attack the board members.

Another student offered me this story: In a fit of rage his wife slapped him. Without thinking, he hit her back with full force, something he later deeply regretted. This response was based on his upbringing; he had been raised on the streets and was very accustomed to getting into brawls. After many years of meditation and becoming aware of his feelings, he realized that, if he were in that situation again, he could choose to act rather than react, and respond differently. The next situation in which he would have automatically gone into his fight response (and physically attacked another person), he took a step back and became aware of all the unpleasant feelings inside him, such as the pressure around his temples, nausea, and tightness around his gut. With his new understanding, he was able to consciously decide how to react, while remaining centered and calm.

Does emotional tranquility have any application in day-to-day life? Emotional tranquility is very powerful in daily life. Malaysian meditation teacher Dr. Thynn Thynn, a mother and doctor juggling real-world challenges, responds to this question:

"Because you no longer struggle with your emotions, you can learn to look at them without judging, clinging to, or rejecting them. They are no longer threatening to you. You learn to relate to your emotions more naturally, like a witness. Even when faced with conflicts and filled with emotions, you view them with equanimity. As you become more stable, you can deal with conflicts without losing your emotional balance."[5]

Personal Encounters with Meditation

Tanya describes herself as a high-achieving career woman who once worked as an equities strategist in an international merchant bank. She also sees herself as a loving perfectionist. She had been in an eight-year relationship with Trevor, in which they had discussed marriage, but Trevor wasn't ready to commit. Tanya ended the relationship, because she did not see any possibility of creating a longer-term relationship and wanted children within the next few years.

"I was really angry at how life had treated me with Trevor. I thought he had just used me all this time. I felt stupid for being in love with him. One day I started getting heart palpitations. I went to the cardiologist, and he assured me that there was nothing wrong with my heart. However, if the symptoms didn't improve, he would need to 'have a look around,' run a camera to my heart through an artery in my leg! Yuck! He advised relaxation, and suggested I speak to a psychologist. I did, and the psychologist recommended meditation. I did the relaxation practice and the calm meditation. It was all good, but nothing earth shattering. I had played sports from an early age and worked hard, so I knew how to deal with stress.

"Then I began doing the emotional tranquility meditation, and wow! That was really hard. I struggled to show love and kindness to myself. As soon as I tried, I noticed I had this extreme tightness in my stomach. When it was time to imagine the person with whom I had difficulties, I naturally thought of Trevor. It was really tough. All the anger, frustration, disappointment — everything — came up. I could not finish the first session; I just had to stand up and get out of there. My heart was racing.

"And it finally dawned on me that my heart palpitations were caused by my anger toward Trevor. I knew I was angry and bitter; however, I had been unaware of the extent it was affecting me or my health. The next time I tried the meditation I used an annoying coworker. This time, the feelings were much more manageable. After a few months I tried using Trevor again. I still felt the same feelings of anger and hurt, but this time I could face them. My heart still raced, and I still unconsciously took shorter breaths when thinking of him.

"I have continued the meditation practice, and I'm still practicing using Trevor as the difficult person. But lately I've found that thinking about him does not have the same effect on me as it did before. The other day he called to wish me a happy birthday, and instead of freezing on the phone I asked about his life; I was okay afterward. Normally this would have put me into a state of depression and anger for a few days. I am dating again, which is nice. One of the great benefits is that I do not need to talk about Trevor in conversation; I think my current dates really appreciate that!"

The main power of the emotional tranquility meditation is that it helps you gain an insight into your emotional land mines as well as your emotional treasure chests, those feelings buried deep within your subconscious. Once you have this awareness, you will develop much more mental clarity.

Emotional tranquility leads to emotional balance, which enhances your mental resilience. If you want to understand why you behave as you do, it is important to be aware of your emotional makeup. When we develop emotional tranquility, new skills become available to us, allowing us to respond to the world with calm and self-control.

We use emotions of love and kindness to develop tranquility. By directing positive emotions toward ourselves, a loved one, a neutral person, and a difficult person, we develop the skill of emotional tranquility. Being aware of our emotional makeup will help us develop mental resilience.

CHAPTER TEN

developing insight

Nothing is more terrible than activity without insight.

THOMAS CARLYLE

INSIGHT IS AWARENESS AND UNDERSTANDING. In its essence, insight meditation is a process by which you gain an understanding, deep within your body, that the world, the people you know, and the events around you — everything — is in a continual state of flux. We are all changing, and this state of flux is the world's only constant!

As you become aware that everything changes, you will sense the preciousness of each moment and want to be more conscious of the present. As you develop deeper levels of insight into the changing nature of the world and everything around you, you will have no other option than to let go of worry and fear of the future and regrets of the past.

Worry does not empty tomorrow of its sorrow;
it empties today of its strength.

CORRIE TEN BOOM

Understanding Insight

Insight has been defined as a clear awareness of exactly what is happening as it happens.[1] Insight is the ability to see clearly and intuitively into the nature of a complex personality or situation. Do you have a clear perception of the world around you? Or, do you know some people with real insight into themselves, who know their strengths and weaknesses, what they are good at and what they need help with? You may notice that such persons also understand that, in life, everything changes. They do not take their successes or failures too seriously; they seem quick to forgive and avoid carrying around a lot emotional hubris.

Or you may have come across people with very little insight. They are the ones who seem to take everything in their lives seriously, losing perspective of what's important and what's not. They seem agitated and anxious a great deal of the time; they find it hard to forgive, and wind up holding on for years to misdeeds done to them.

It's hard to explain precisely what insight is. It's similar to trying to explain what water is experientially as opposed to its chemical makeup. You could say that water is a clear liquid made up of two hydrogen atoms and one oxygen atom. You could describe the things one can do with water, but that description is very inadequate. The only way to understand water is to experience it. Try giving a very thirsty person a nice cool glass of water on a hot day. As soon as the feelings of elation and relief from the quenching of all thirst come, that person will understand. In the same way, insight must be experienced rather than merely described.

Learning about Insight Meditation

Essentially insight meditation is the practice of investigative personal discovery. It is a further stage in your developing meditation practice. This meditation technique teaches us how to develop an insight into ourselves, particularly the transient nature of our feelings, problems, perceptions, and, ultimately, physical lives. This brings a perspective of freshness, freedom, and understanding that the actual elements of life that create pleasure or displeasure and success or failure are continually changing. Our perceptions of these elements are also in a state of constant flux. We might understand intellectually that our lives mean constant change, but we also may understand it at an emotional level.

To some degree, we continually search for certainty in our careers, relationships, health, and finances. This craving for certainty stops us from living a full life of courage and freedom. This desire for stability or certainty stops us from looking for a more satisfying career or taking chances in a new or long-term relationship, and makes us cling to our youth and bemoan growing older. All this fear can rob us of passion. However, change is the natural process of life.

Most of us do not accept, or even believe in, the continual flux of life. However strange this may seem, once we truly accept this at a *physical* level, we will not need to search for certainty.

Insight meditation aims to bring about a deep knowledge of what affects your body and an acceptance that everything changes in your body. (What mystics and meditators have known for many centuries, quantum physicists, mathematicians, and biologists are now discovering. For an entertaining description of this, check out the film *What the Bleep Do We Know!?*) In knowing this, instead of being driven to seek certainty in your life, you will allow yourself to live more freely. This will remove any fear of the future, hence reducing your stress.

> *What lies before us, what lies behind us,*
> *is nothing compared to what lies within us.*
>
> RALPH WALDO EMERSON

The Importance of Insight Meditation

Wouldn't it be great to develop insights into ourselves? Insight is important because, with it, you are much less likely to suffer. Of course, this doesn't mean that you magically will be spared all of life's inevitable challenges or pain. But you will understand this very important principle: pain is inevitable; suffering is optional.

As you tackle the tribulations of life, insight helps you refrain from taking yourself, your challenges, and life itself too seriously, because you will know that no matter what situation you are in, good or bad, it will change. This insight into the changing nature of the world will give you equanimity and joy.

> *There are only two tragedies in life:*
> *not getting what you want, and getting what you want.*
>
> OSCAR WILDE

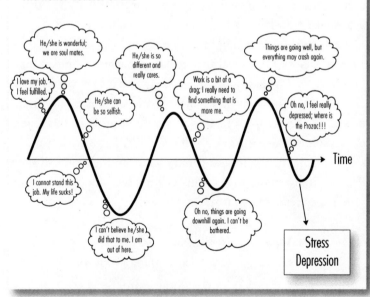

The Roller Coaster of Life

The preceding diagram shows the variety of a typical person's thoughts. All humans experience ups and downs, certainties and fears, and successes and challenges. Sometimes relationships work, and our finances and careers go well, so we feel elated. And then, inevitably, there is change. Relationships sour, careers stumble, and we lose money. In extreme situations, on the downward slide we experience stress, depression, and anxiety.

The skill necessary to keep afloat and avoid sinking into depression or hopelessness is insight. With insight meditation, despite experiencing our own changing nature, we can start developing joy and equanimity. So, while the ups and downs never go away, we reduce our perceptions of their amplitude and uncover the joy of being alive so that we can enjoy the journey.

Another business analogy is the way savvy stock-market investors face the changing fortunes of the market. What makes them savvy, and what is their expertise? They know that markets go up and down and change is constant. These investors make gains over the longer term because they do not jump in and out at the wrong time. They buy when the nervous sell, and vice versa.

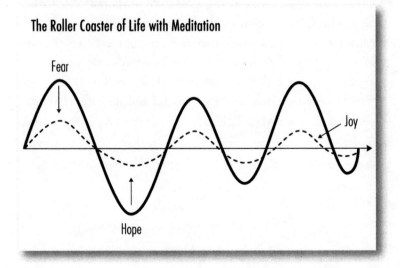

The Roller Coaster of Life with Meditation

Fear

Joy

Hope

Great stock investors have a sense of equanimity. They don't get overly flustered when they lose money or when they make it. They follow the long-term trends rather than try to make money from daily fluctuations.

Security is mostly a superstition. It does not exist in nature,
nor do the children of men, as a whole, experience it.
Avoiding danger is no safer in the long run than outright exposure.
Life is either a daring adventure or nothing.

HELEN KELLER

How else can insight help? Imagine that you are worried about the future: you fear losing your job or putting on weight, you can't find the right house, or your partner has threatened to leave you. Most of us would respond to these situations and thoughts with a sense of distress and angst. Now, with the profound insight that you are continually changing, imagine yourself able to recognize that such seemingly drastic events are not so bad and not permanent. The future you, the person you will be next year, will probably be different from the person you are this year. This future person will be able to cope differently than you can now. So it makes no sense to worry about what might happen to the future you. A word of caution: It's easy to say or read this kind of material and intellectualize it. However, that is really different from living it, which takes practice and patience. I have met very few people, myself included, who can truly do this in all areas of their lives. A prominent meditation teacher said, "I have spent seventeen years of my life learning how to live in the present moment."

You can never step in the same river twice.

HERACLITUS

Beginning to Develop Insight

This is the fourth stage in your practice. You have experienced calm and emotional tranquility in the previous stages. I hope that during your practice you have experienced moments of pure quiet and real tranquility. In this stage you will look deep within to access insight about yourself.

Mental Resilience Training Audio: Track 4 — Insight

Track 4 is a guided insight meditation. In this practice we will notice our bodily sensations to develop insight into ourselves.

The Steps to Insight

STEP 1: Assume your meditation posture and bring awareness to the sensations at the tip of your nose as you breathe. Stay with these sensations until you can maintain your concentration for a period of at least five breaths.

STEP 2: Scan your body from your toes to your head. The focus of insight meditation is to scan the body for sensations. First, we start at our feet. We notice the sensations in our feet, then our legs, thighs, buttocks, and so on, gradually scanning upward toward the head. Allow your focus to stay with the sensations, not only big sensations, such as an ache in your knee, but on each and every sensation that arises. Once you have scanned all the way up through your head, move up and down the body, and precisely notice the sensations and feelings, labeling them *pleasant, unpleasant,* or *neutral* if you like. Then move on.

STEP 3: Scan your body starting at your head and moving down to your toes, in the opposite direction to that of step 2. Your challenge is to objectively observe yourself. Whenever you feel a sensation, try to avoid enhancing it if it feels good or running away from it if it feels unpleasant. It is also important to remain engaged even when there's a neutral feeling; just notice the feeling and realize that sensations come and go. The goal here is to become aware of the extent to which your body is in a state of flux. Keep your attention moving. Some of the sensations might be big and heavy while others feel light and tingly.

Often, when you least expect it, you will get glimpses of insight. These flashes can be a perception that you might have previously regarded blindingly obvious; however, they can be extremely profound. After a flash of insight, your life is never the same again! Now, if that sounds like a huge claim, think about this: Remember how the first time you had an earth-shattering realization (perhaps when you realized Santa Claus was not real?) changed the way you thought about your life. Well, with an insight, no matter how much you try to convince yourself, you cannot go back to your old way of thinking. (Life-changing insights are not unique to meditation; many people have experienced them when undergoing psychotherapy, Neuro-Linguistic Programming [NLP], and Focusing, to name a few modalities.) Or what about the first time you realized that your parents were real, fallible people just like you.

Once you have an insight, it is with you forever. It is something you can draw on and use for the rest of your life. Your level of calm may fluctuate depending on how much meditation you do, but your insight will grow. This insight into yourself and your way of reacting to things will keep on developing.

Frequently Asked Questions

A lot of different feelings arise as I practice meditation, causing me confusion. Not all of them are pleasant. Shouldn't meditation make me feel better? One of the insights you may encounter concerns how you experience and process feelings. As you sit in meditation, many feelings will arise, sometimes pleasant, unpleasant, and neutral feelings almost one after the other. Do not be alarmed or try to force them away. They will come and go, and feeling them is a significant part of the meditation. Most people spend their lives trying to create (or re-create) good feelings and run away from bad ones. This running causes a lot of our tension and stress, but a great deal of peace comes when you realize that you can never have only good feelings, nor will you always have bad feelings. Everything just comes and goes.

> *When I repress my emotions, my stomach keeps score.*
> JOHN POWELL

Why are we focusing on insight rather than calm? I was enjoying getting calmer. Insight is a very powerful milestone in meditation. Realistically insight is the goal, and calm is the means. When you become calm and tranquil, your mind will settle. As you start seeing through what was once muddy water, your life will become clearer. The most surprising, or the most insightful, realizations about yourself will actually come from within you.

These insights can be very dramatic and powerful. They may radically change your life, sometimes seemingly instantaneously. But of course, it isn't an instant process. I like the metaphor of water coming to a boil. When you heat a pot of water, it takes a while to come to a boil. The water doesn't seem to move for a few minutes; despite the rising heat, the water appears still to the naked eye. Then, at a certain temperature it starts to boil rapidly. This very dramatic reaction was in process for a while, but the evidence of it seems instantaneous. In the same way, you may sit for meditation every day with no major insight, and then one day, bang!

You will achieve some insight, and it will change your life forever. Life will never be the same again.

Of course, it does not always happen that way. For some, it is a gradual development. Many people experience great insights during meditation retreats, probably partly because those going on such retreats are in an intense period in their lives.

My experience confirms this. On one of my ten-day meditation retreats, nothing happened for the first seven days. Then, after the seventh day, I was astounded at how much bubbled up; it was given the space to do so once my mental chatter became quiet. I became acutely aware of my thought processes. It truly felt like a magical experience. As I have gone deeper in my practice, I have come to the conclusion that meditation can be magical and profound, but also a very ordinary and grounding experience.

Why do we use physical sensations to develop insight into ourselves? This sounds a bit like hocus-pocus. We concentrate on the body in insight meditation, because every thought or emotion we have produces a chemical and physiological reaction.[2] If you tell a lie, there will be an immediate change in your heart rate. The lie-detector polygraph test uses this basic principle. Think about how many lies you might tell in a day; for example, instead of honestly expressing how you feel, you might say, "I'm fine, thanks." Or you might fudge the numbers a little when filling out your weight on a form. All these seemingly minute fibs add up, causing stress to accumulate in your body.

Insight meditation acknowledges that stress. Through this technique we listen to the body as a mechanism for listening to the mind. Through the nexus between mind and body, we can open up what's inside our minds by paying attention to the sensations and feelings in our bodies.

This is a technique that has been used in many Eastern philosophies for hundreds, even thousands, of years. In modern culture, which embraces psychotherapy as a valid way to access the mind, practitioners who research the mind-body connection have corroborated many of Eastern philosophy's techniques.

One psychotherapist in particular, Eugene Gendlin, mastered a technique called Focusing in his quest to understand why only a small percentage of patients of particular forms of psychotherapy had sustained success. After his research team videotaped thousands of hours of psychotherapy sessions, a very important observation emerged: Gendlin concluded that only when patients were able to identify their psychological traumas in their bodies were they able to let them go and continue with their lives. Eugene Gendlin called this a "felt sense."[3] (Strangely enough, this was the same instruction my meditation master gave me. Unfortunately he did not have access to the technology or statistical sampling techniques to convince me of his argument!)

> *Our own physical body possesses a wisdom,*
> *which we who inhabit the body lack.*
>
> HENRY MILLER

To release blocked emotions, all we have to do is relax. It may sound simple, but we know it isn't. However, it is a skill we can develop relatively easily. As we relax and become physically still, we become aware of the sensations in the body. These sensations represent emotions long locked inside us that have started bubbling up to the surface. If you observe the coming and going of these emotions, they lose their power over you. On the other hand, if you stop observing and start thinking about or reacting against a sensation, you become more entangled, and the pull of that emotion becomes stronger. The insight here is that nothing is permanent. The good feeling goes, and the bad feeling goes; like your breath, nothing is ever really stationary.

Sometimes we try to get rid of unpleasant feelings by getting rid of circumstances, to the point of blaming people around us for creating them. How many people jump from job to job or partner to partner in attempts to eliminate unpleasant feelings? They do not ask the right questions, which might be, "What would I like to contribute in my job?" or "What am I expecting to give in my relationship?" Rather, they go from situation to situation, blaming others, such as organizations and partners, for their unhappiness. If they were to really investigate their feelings — "I've got this feeling inside of me; let me look at it; let me observe it" — their patterns of pain or dissatisfaction might diminish or even disappear.

Whether related to alcohol, drugs, or food, addictive behavior is often an attempt to run away from uncomfortable feelings by indulging in physical gratification. If we can notice the feelings and become more comfortable with their very existence, then we do not need to mask them or, indeed, compulsively chase a pleasurable feeling.

Of course, running to and from feelings can be very tiring. One of the deepest benefits you can get from meditation is to realize the real beauty in merely observing feelings and letting them come and go. The force of such an insight really changes how you live your life.

You may have heard of people who have gone through a life-changing event, such as being diagnosed with a life-threatening illness, speak about their lives in terms of before and after the incident. They talk about life "before I got cancer" or "before I had the car accident." My life-changing event was the death of our first child. I regard my whole life as "before" and "after," and doing so has really brought me insight about what is important. A similar flash of insight can occur continually when you meditate.

After the calming meditation I felt great, but now I feel more agitated. Why? Many meditators experience this. Of course, you would want things to get more and more pleasant and easy. Let me reassure you; it takes time. If you have a painful boil on your skin, you can apply an anesthetic to dull the pain, and it will only trouble you for a while. This is analogous to calming meditation techniques. If you really want to get rid of the source of that pain, you need to lance it, and that hurts! But once you face that pain, you will have lasting relief. Insight meditation is like this; it opens up areas in your mind and releases the pain inside.

Do certain sensations mean something? I seem to feel tightness in my throat. You will notice sensations coming and going from your body without any obvious reason. They can pass as waves of uneasiness, tingling, itchiness, pain, numbness, and so on. When you start meditation practice, the sensations feel coarse and unpleasant. As you continue practicing, the sensations feel more refined. The body frees itself of anxiety, and you feel moments of bliss because the gateway opens between the conscious and subconscious minds. This is possible because you are calm, tranquil, and relaxed.

However, you should be aware that it's really hard to sit in one spot as these sensations rise up. You may feel like scratching an itch or moving away from the discomfort. Some people get to this stage and worry that they have ruined the process somewhere along the way. They had reached a point where they felt calm and tranquil, and then, bang! They feel uncomfortable and restless again. You are getting deep into your subconscious, and all the negative emotions have become physically noticeable. By observing and letting go of them, you are hitting a milestone.

Does having equanimity mean being indifferent or apathetic to life and what's happening in the world? Many of my students ask whether equanimity means apathy or indifference. This is not the case.

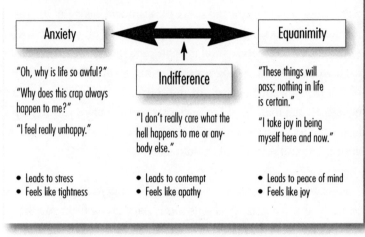

Equanimity vs. Anxiety

Anxiety		Equanimity
"Oh, why is life so awful?"	Indifference	"These things will pass; nothing in life is certain."
"Why does this crap always happen to me?"		
"I feel really unhappy."	"I don't really care what the hell happens to me or anybody else."	"I take joy in being myself here and now."
• Leads to stress • Feels like tightness	• Leads to contempt • Feels like apathy	• Leads to peace of mind • Feels like joy

Equanimity is a joyous feeling, on the opposite end of the spectrum from anxiety. Indifference lies somewhere in between but feels completely different. When indifferent, you are not engaged with the world. Equanimity is similar to knowing that there are seasons in our lives. It cannot always be spring or summer; we all have to go through our winters, when it becomes cold and dark. We all have blue days, but we can experience joy even in those, which helps our bodies and minds regenerate. With equanimity, you perceive this joy as an acceptance that it gets cold in the winter and hot and sweaty in the summer, and each has its pleasures and pains. With equanimity you will find joy in your cold, dark emotions, just as you do in your warm, light ones. Equanimity will naturally emerge from the clarity you experience as your mind regains its natural resilience and radiance.

Equanimity comes from the realization that everything changes. Sometimes things can be good, and sometimes they can be bad. The real skill is in how we give meaning to events in our lives based on our chosen perceptions of them.

IS THAT SO?

Once upon a time, a pretty unmarried girl in the village fell pregnant. Her parents became very angry, demanding that she tell them who the father was. The girl was frightened and embarrassed about her predicament, and eager to get the heat off her, so she implicated a famous spiritual master who lived in the village. The master was respected for his very austere and pure life. The angry parents confronted the spiritual master and told him of their daughter's confession. When asked to respond, the master remarked, "Is that so?" After that, the village scorned the master for being a hypocrite, but he maintained his equanimity.

After a few months the child was born, and the new grandparents brought the child to the master, demanding that he look after the infant. When they handed over the child, the master again remarked, "Is that so?" The master gave up his intense spiritual practices and devoted his energy to the child; he became an exemplary father, anticipating all of the child's needs.

A few months later the child's mother became wracked with guilt and remorse for what she had done. One day she confessed to her parents the real identity of the father, a young man in the village. The grandparents rushed to the spiritual master and apologetically asked for the child back. Without blinking, the master remarked, "Is that so?" and returned the child, bidding the grandparents well.

The master did not complain when he was accused, because he knew that life is always in a state of flux. He loved the baby unconditionally, but when it was time to give the child back, he did so with honor and respect, without being attached.

My master first taught me this story to illustrate how we must always love unconditionally, remaining detached, and how things always change in life.

Personal Encounters with Meditation

Betty is a successful career woman. By her own estimation, she has a great life: she is one of very few female partners in a large international law firm, has a good relationship with her husband, and is extremely healthy.

However, she often feels that something in her life is not quite right. She has a constant sense that she is on trial and is only as good as her last achievement. She decides to take up meditation because she has heard that it might calm her and increase her performance.

"I got a lot out of it, and felt calmer and clearer, but after sitting for a few months, I decided to go on an extended meditation retreat. I sat for the first couple of days, and it was really calming and relaxing. Then, on the third day, something quite amazing happened; something suddenly clicked. I realized that, my whole life, I had always tried to be good at something. When I was young I wanted to be a great daughter to my parents. Then I wanted to be a great student. Later I wanted to be a great wife, and then I wanted to be a great mother. At work I wanted to be the highest-earning partner. I realized that my whole life had been driven by fear of failing at whatever was before me. I had been driven by fear, a fear of being unloved by the people around me unless I fulfilled certain roles. This was a negative emotion that had driven me and generated my deep, constant sense of anxiety. It seemed like a flash of illumination; it was staggering. But even though it was a dramatic insight, it did not change my life overnight. Nevertheless, my awareness allowed me to start considering how I could approach life from a more positive emotion than the fear of failure.

"I still do what I did before, but I feel much lighter. I do the things I do because I feel joy when I am a good mother, partner, and lawyer, not because I am trying to win love from people. I definitely feel lighter. The stresses of daily activities have lifted. Also I am much kinder to myself. If I am not the partner with the highest revenues in a year, I'm no longer hard on myself. If I miss an occasional school event, I don't think I am a failure as a mother. Now I feel I am much less an insecure overachiever, and more a person driven by the need to bring joy into my life and those of the people around me. I feel that I know what I want and no longer have to satisfy everybody else, mistakenly thinking it will satisfy me. Is this self-realization? I don't know, but I do know that I have realized what is important to me.

"One key piece of insight for me is that my life will always be in a state of flux. My relationships with myself, my partner, my work, my kids, and my parents are always changing. They are changing, and I am changing. I cannot expect my love for my husband to be the same as when we first started dating. So I am going to stop trying to force him and myself to feel a certain way about our relationship. It's still wonderful, but it has changed over the years of our marriage. The love I have for my kids is changing. So I am going to let them slowly go on their own journeys rather than try to hold onto them as long as I can.

"I used to know this in my head; now I feel that I believe it with my heart. I think I am almost at the stage where I can feel it in my body. So I have stopped struggling to keep things as I think they 'should be' while fearing change. I now know that this is the way it's going to be, and I need to live with it."

David: Pain is inevitable; suffering is optional.

David is an outstanding athlete with hopes of a professional football career and a plan to eventually become a sportswriter. One day he is involved in a car accident that wipes out any possibility of competing professionally. David takes up meditation during his recuperation process.

"I was in a lot of pain; there was no doubt about that. Being in sports meant you got used to pain. I understood pain, but this pain was different. There was so much more involved now; I could not stop thinking about what could have been. I took up meditation because somebody told me I could better manage my pain. I did not want to end up a painkiller junkie, and that was slowly where I was headed. During meditation I had some amazing insights. When I stopped the mental chattering, I noticed the pain was still there; that did not change. But I felt it was not as bad as before. Then one day it hit me really hard. I realized my suffering was not due to the pain but to the stories I had been telling myself of how shitty and unfair it was that my life had been so badly turned around.

"The pain is still there, but I am much better at understanding and responding to it. I take painkillers when it gets really bad. But without the sad stories going around in my head, my life is much easier. I still have to face the challenges of the future, but I won't spend as much energy feeling sorry for myself."

No two people have the same experiences. Therefore our experiences during insight meditation will be unique. However, with this in mind, the experience of letting go of emotional baggage will be very liberating.

The power of meditation is the power of nonjudgmental observation. And in insight meditation, we practice being nonjudgmental toward ourselves. Insight meditation can sometimes be confronting. We allow ourselves to reach different levels of sensation within our psyches and our bodies, and thus achieve a deeper understanding of how we are in the world.

We access insight through sensations in our bodies. As we practice insight meditation we develop equanimity, which will not remove life's challenges but will allow us to approach them from a different perspective.

CHAPTER ELEVEN

cultivating wisdom

Knowing others is intelligence; knowing yourself is true wisdom.
Mastering others is strength; mastering yourself is true power.

ANONYMOUS

WHAT DOES WISDOM MEAN TO YOU? If you look around at people you know and admire, you can detect those who are wise. We are naturally attracted to these people. Their wisdom can forge significant changes in the organizations we work with or even the world. These people are different. They do not have the same fears that drive the majority of the population. They act with integrity from their own values and are willing to stick to those values no matter what the consequence.

There may have been times when you, too, felt wise, perhaps a time when you were clear about what you wanted to achieve and what drove you toward your goals. The decisions made with such clarity are the ones that stand the test of time.

Though it is useful to consider wisdom, I feel that wisdom cannot be acquired from a book. But we can touch upon the wisdom that comes from meditation, providing yet another reason to develop mental resilience.

Knowledge can be communicated, but wisdom cannot.

HERMANN HESSE

Understanding Wisdom

Wisdom has been defined as navigational intelligence. Mariners know the importance of finding their bearings before starting a voyage. We all have to know our own North Star. Once we have identified it, we can make progress toward our destination. Wisdom can also be considered the ability to make the choices that create the positive consequences we want in our lives.[1] It is a kind of clarity to facilitate making effective choices and decisions. Without this wisdom we are at the whims of others' needs, instructions, or expectations.

In the context of meditation, we can gain wisdom only by asking questions and not forcing the answers, but waiting for them to arise. (This does sound somewhat esoteric or Zenlike, as in the conundrum, "What is the sound of one hand clapping?" At the end of the day, wisdom is experiential and therefore difficult to convey with words.) How does this happen? Going back to our metaphor of the glass filled with muddy water, after a period of settling down, the water becomes absolutely clear. If you then shine a flashlight through that glass of water, you start to see clearly. This is when answers appear.

When you ask yourself, "Why am I here? What's the meaning of life? What does my life really mean?" you may start getting a different response than more conventional answers such as "to be somebody's parent" or "to be somebody's husband, wife, child, brother, sister, or friend." You begin to understand what you want from your own existence. After meditation the mind becomes resilient and resembles a mirror, reflecting thoughts and sensations while remaining untouched by them. The luster of the mirror with

its ability to reflect the continual changes of life remains unchanged.

We do not receive wisdom; we must discover it for ourselves,
after a journey through the wilderness, which no one else can make
for us, which no one can spare us; for our wisdom is the point of view
from which we come at last to regard the world.

MARCEL PROUST

The wisdom gained from meditation is not one size fits all;
some call it enlightenment. While many people take enlightenment very seriously, the best definition of enlightenment I have
heard is deceptively simple: the ability to lighten up. A meditation teacher I respect greatly, Ayya Khema, a German Jew who
fled the Nazis, explained it like this: "Enlightenment is like playing a game with a child. You get involved with them, you cele-
brate the victories, and you mourn the losses. However, you know,
always, that it is a game. As you play, you do not feel the stress of
the game, knowing you can step back from it anytime."[2]

We have heard the phrase "life is just a game" many times,
but how much do we really believe or practice it? If we really experienced it, how would it affect our level of stress? What if, in
your body twenty-four hours a day, you truly felt that this life is
just a game? What if you believed that everything you did —
every achievement, every relationship, every thought you had —
was just part of a game?

Imagine playing a game of Monopoly with a child. You feel
excited and passionate about the game, and you enjoy the child's
involvement. You play with an open heart, knowing full well that
you will walk away from the game without consequence. There's
no reality associated with it, so there's no stress, although there's
a lot of fun and even a bit of tension.

In the same way, once you gain the wisdom that life is a game, you will look at it differently, even if the components of your life are the same. One of my favorite traditional Zen sayings is this: "Before enlightenment, chop wood, carry water; after enlightenment, chop wood, carry water."

Turning to our modern lives, we might say, "Before enlightenment, attend meetings, give presentations, engage in relationships, live healthfully; after enlightenment, attend meetings, give presentations, engage in relationships, live healthfully." With enlightenment, the silt in the glass is still there, but it has settled! What you do looks very much the same. However, your perception of life is significantly different.

LOVE: AIKIDO IN COMBAT
by Terry Dobson, Aikido Master

The train rattled through the suburbs of Tokyo on a spring afternoon. Our car was comparatively empty, a few housewives with kids in tow and some old folks going shopping. At one station the doors opened, and suddenly the afternoon quiet was shattered by a man bellowing violent, incomprehensible curses.

He staggered into our car wearing laborer's clothing. He was big, drunk, and dirty. Screaming, he swung at a woman holding a baby. The blow sent her spinning into the laps of an elderly couple.

Terrified, the couple jumped up and scrambled toward the other end of the car. The laborer aimed a kick at the retreating old woman's back but missed as she scuttled to safety. This so enraged the drunk that he grabbed the metal pole in the center of the car and tried to wrench it out of its stanchion. The train lurched ahead, the passengers frozen in fear. I stood up. I was young then, some twenty years ago, and in pretty good shape. I'd put in eight hours of aikido training almost daily for three years. I liked to throw and grapple. Trouble was, my martial arts skills were untested in actual combat.

As students of aikido, we were not allowed to fight. "Aikido," my teacher had said again and again, "is the art of reconciliation. Whoever has the mind to fight has broken his connection with the universe. If you try to dominate people, you are already defeated. We study how to resolve conflict, not how to start it."

I listened to his words. I even went so far as to cross the street to avoid the *chimpira*, the pinball punks who lounge around train stations. I felt both tough and holy. However, in my heart I wanted an absolutely legitimate opportunity to save the innocent by destroying the guilty. "This is it!" I declared, getting to my feet. People are in danger, and if I don't do something fast, they will probably get hurt.

Seeing me, the drunk saw his chance to focus his rage. "Aha!" he roared. "A foreigner! You need a lesson in Japanese manners!" I held on lightly to the commuter strap overhead and gave him a slow look of disgust and dismissal. I pursed my lips and blew him an insolent kiss.

"All right!" he hollered. "You're gonna get a lesson." He gathered himself for a rush at me.

During the split second in which he prepared to make his move, someone shouted, "Hey!"

It was ear splitting. I wheeled to my left, and the drunk spun to his right. We both stared down at a little old Japanese man, well into his seventies, a tiny gentleman, immaculate in his kimono. He took no notice of me but beamed delightedly at the laborer. "C'mere," the old man beckoned to the drunk. "C'mere and talk with me."

He waved his hand lightly. The big man followed, as if on a string. He planted his feet belligerently in front of the old gentleman, demanding, "Why the hell should I talk to you?"

The old man continued, "What'cha been drinkin'?"

"I been drinkin' sake," the laborer bellowed back, "and it's none of your business!"

"Okay, that's wonderful," the old man said, "absolutely wonderful! You see, I love sake too. Every night, me and my wife (she's seventy-six, you know), we warm up a little bottle of sake and take it out into the garden, where we sit on an old wooden bench. We watch the sun go down, and look to see how our persimmon tree is doing. My great-grandfather planted that tree, and we worry about whether it will recover from those ice storms we had last winter. We take our sake and go out to enjoy the evening, even when it rains!" He looked up at the laborer, eyes twinkling.

As he struggled to follow the old man's conversation, the drunk's face began to soften. His fists slowly unclenched.

"Yeah," he said, "I love persimmons too..." His voice trailed off.

"Yes," said the old man, smiling, "and I'm sure you have a wonderful wife."

"No," replied the laborer, "my wife died." Very gently, swaying with the motion of the train, the big man began to sob. "I don't got no wife, I don't got no home, I don't got no job. I am so ashamed of myself." Tears rolled down his cheeks, and a spasm of despair rippled through his body.

Now it was my turn. Standing there in well-scrubbed, youthful innocence, in my make-this-world-safe-for-democracy righteousness, I suddenly felt dirtier than he was. When the train arrived at my stop, the doors opened, and I heard the old man cluck sympathetically, "My, my, that is a difficult predicament indeed. Sit down here and tell me about it."

I turned for one last look. The laborer was sprawled on the seat with his head in the old man's lap. The old man was softly stroking the drunk's filthy, matted hair.

I sat down on a bench. What I had wanted to do with muscle had been accomplished with kind words. I had just witnessed aikido applied in combat, and the essence of it was love.[3]

The Benefits of Wisdom

You may have come across people in life who have innate wisdom. They seem to have a flow, a presence, and a kindness about everything they do. They can be kind when others are not. They seem to truly live rather than exist. And they radiate understanding. Their wisdom allows them to make good decisions about how to live their lives.

Particularly in business, one makes much better decisions with this sense of wisdom, not always better in the sense of a greater return on investment but because decisions are based on a core set of human values.

Consider for a moment the power that many businesspeople have to do good or, indeed, to do harm. We all see the evidence of harmful practices — harmful to people (defective, dangerous products or risky work practices), the environment (toxic chemicals disrupting our endocrine systems and CO_2 warming our planet), and democracy (lives compromised by exploitation) — that businesses have inflicted, all with the justification that they are achieving the greatest profits for their shareholders.

Now consider what might happen if the executives that run these businesses had wisdom, the wisdom to take a long-term view and say, "No. I understand that profits are important, but I also have the wisdom to guide my business to serve the shareholders *and* the community." Would we have experienced the commercial and environmental disasters inflicted by companies such as Enron or Union Carbide had more wisdom been employed? What if our CEOs could make decisions with the kind of wisdom displayed by the old man on the train?

Consider the power in parents' and educators' ability to change the world we live in. Consider what would happen if the people with that type of responsibility could approach their tasks with wisdom and tranquility. Imagine if they had the tranquility of the monks walking across the rice paddies during gunfire, as described by David Busch in chapter 9. Could this be the beginning of the end of senseless violence?

Beginning to Cultivate Wisdom

This is the final stage in your practice. Fundamentally this stage is about flowing with whatever happens, using the focus and peace you have developed from previous stages.

Mental Resilience Training Audio:
Track 5 — Wisdom Meditation

Wisdom begins in wonder.

SOCRATES

This part of meditation practice is very personal. Each of us has to find our own way to achieve wisdom.

Think again about the glass of muddy water. Just let it sit until the sediment goes to the bottom. Similarly, sit and observe your thoughts, your breath, and the sensations in your body. Do not try to concentrate. Do not try to block any of your thoughts. Just be aware of your mind, remaining in a state of wonder about all that emerges and disappears.

There are no explicit steps to achieving wisdom. All that one can do is be aware and stay in a state of wonder for the duration of the meditation. Sit, observe, and be open to and interested in whatever may arise.

Frequently Asked Question

What is the best and quickest way to develop wisdom? We should not speed through meditation, because the process requires slowing down. To enhance your meditation practice you may consider going on a meditation retreat, somewhere away from the busyness of daily life. Give yourself some time to let the sediment settle.

Not only can periods of intensive meditation, such as you might enjoy at a retreat, help strengthen your meditation practice, but they can also help when you are poised to make an important decision in your life, such as choosing a partner, making a big investment, or deciding when to retire or sell your business. Take time to think about yourself, but refrain from considering the pros and cons involved in the decision. Instead do the opposite: let go of your thoughts. Following the retreat, you probably will have the mental clarity and wisdom to make the right decision.

The calm that you experience in meditation will come and go. Naturally, the more you meditate, the less mental chatter you will experience. Also naturally, if you stop meditating, you will feel less calm. However, wisdom and insight will never dissipate. Just as you never forget how to ride a bike regardless of wavering fitness levels, you will not lose your ability to tap into your insight and wisdom once you have learned how.

Wisdom is not information but an abiding presence, an intuitive, sensing opening of the body and heart. In wisdom the body of fear drops away and our heart comes to rest. Like love, wisdom needs no explanation.

JACK KORNFIELD

Personal Encounters with Meditation

Andrew is a successful mathematician and fund manager. For him, life is all about rigor and accuracy; everything needs to sit right. He needs everything in his life to be perfect and even describes himself as a perfectionist. If anything in his surroundings is slightly off kilter, his stress level skyrockets. He has been led to meditation because of high blood pressure and the fear of a potential heart attack. He knows he needs to take life a bit less seriously, but he just hasn't found the right mechanism to help him do that. He has been to counselors and taken strong blood-pressure medication, but wants something else.

"I came to meditation because I thought it would help me relax. In the beginning, meditation was not about relaxation at all. I found it excruciatingly painful to sit still. I thought of the 101 things I had on my task list. Closing my eyelids without fidgeting seemed like being in self-imposed solitary confinement. I still remember the first meditation sitting. I thought the bell would never go off. I couldn't believe ten minutes could take that long.

"As I practiced, something really bizarre happened. I felt as if

I were going deeper into myself. I actually started to look forward to my meditation sessions. I found that they were a bit of a relief from the stuff swirling around in my head. Changes started to happen to me in and out of meditation. I basically stopped being so task focused. Instead of getting pleasure from just checking off the things on my task list, I actually tried to start enjoying doing whatever I had to do during my day. When I thought of the things I needed to do, I felt detached from the outcome. Sure, I gave it my very best, but I was not so anxious about the outcome. I started living rather than merely existing until the next deadline.

"My wife noticed the difference and summed it up as my willingness to let life take its own course and release myself of being so responsible for the outcome. I cared about the outcome, but I realized there was only so much I could do to influence it. It was like watching an interesting movie without worrying about how it ends. The funny thing is that, since I was more focused on the process than the result, the result generally turned out better. The wisdom I feel I have received is the wisdom of letting go. It is okay to let go."

Catherine: Wisdom is knowing that peace is never far away.

Catherine is the CEO of a large listed company. As she puts it, she got to the top by "being 50 percent smarter and working 100 percent harder than everybody else.

"The biggest wisdom that I have gained from meditating for eight years is that peace is never very far away. After a messy divorce, work pressures, and stomach cancer, I knew I needed to change my life, so I started meditation. Now I know that no matter how crazy life gets, peace is only a few breaths away. This gives me great confidence, because I know that if everything disappeared — my career, my wealth, and my relationships — I could still be content within myself. I recently went on a two-week retreat with no modern conveniences or friends around me. I was amazed that I was just happy being me, not trying to achieve anything or run away from anything — just being me. I am starting to accept myself for who I am.

"My relationships have improved significantly. My boyfriend tells me that I share my own happiness with him rather than look to him to provide my happiness. Only recently have I learned how to enjoy the fruits of my labor without worrying about who is out to get me or which milestone I need to reach before I turn fifty."

The wisdom that comes from meditation is already inside us. In meditation we stop the mental chatter so that we can become aware of this wisdom. The gateways open up in our minds, allowing us to access wisdom. We then continue to live our lives with a set of values that guides our actions.

How does one access this profound wisdom and use it? Really, it's the wisdom of millions of years that has brought us, as human beings, to this stage of development. There is wisdom in our bodies and minds that can bring us great peace to heal ourselves mentally and physically. Wisdom cannot be taught, but it can be experienced. Being still, being aware, and remaining in a state of wonder are the foundation of wisdom in meditation.

CHAPTER TWELVE

bringing it all together

Life is both dreadful and wonderful.
To practice meditation is to be in touch with both aspects.

THICH NHAT HANH

IF YOU HAVE COME THIS FAR IN THE BOOK, you probably have sat in meditation for a few sessions. The purpose of this chapter is to help you keep your practice vibrant.

Developing a
Mental Resilience Training Program

To really make your meditation practice come alive, you need to follow a meditation program. The following twenty-one-day Mental Resilience Training program will help you kick off your practice. If you follow it, you will definitely experience the benefits of meditation. Once you've been on the program for three weeks, you may decide that some of the meditations suit you better than others, and you can choose which meditation technique to follow, depending on your state of mind.

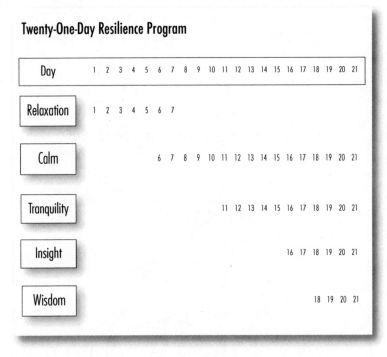

Twenty-One-Day Resilience Program

	1	2	3	4	5	6	7	8	9	10	11	12	13	14	15	16	17	18	19	20	21
Day	1	2	3	4	5	6	7	8	9	10	11	12	13	14	15	16	17	18	19	20	21
Relaxation	1	2	3	4	5	6	7														
Calm						6	7	8	9	10	11	12	13	14	15	16	17	18	19	20	21
Tranquility											11	12	13	14	15	16	17	18	19	20	21
Insight																16	17	18	19	20	21
Wisdom																		18	19	20	21

Beginning Your Meditation Program

The following program runs for three weeks (twenty-one days) and will progressively take you through all the guided meditations.

Start with the guided relaxation (track 1 of the audio) on day 1 and practice it for seven days. Pick a time of day, preferably in the morning, before you start your day, or early evening. If you have time I strongly recommend that you practice twice a day.

On day 6 of your program, start the meditative calm meditation (track 2) in conjunction with the relaxation meditation. On day 11 start the emotional tranquility training (track 3), on day 16 start the insight meditation (track 4), and on day 18 start the wisdom meditation (track 5).

If you find yourself agitated for any reason, you may choose to practice the calm meditation every day for the full twenty-one days.

Overcoming Obstacles

As you meditate, you may experience some obstacles along the way. As in the rest of your life, it's important to find balance in your meditation practice. You may need to make some adjustments to balance how sleepy or restless your mind gets.

The following table shows you why you may experience sleepiness or agitation. If you find yourself nodding off in your meditation, try to eat a bit less before starting, wear lighter clothes, try keeping the lights on in the room, and exercise a little before starting.

Causes of Sleepy or Disturbed Mind

	Sleepy Mind	Disturbed Mind
FOOD	• Overeating • Heavy foods — potatoes, pasta, meat	• Too little • Acidic and spicy • Just vegetables
DRINK	• Milk • Alcohol	• Coffee • Tea
WEATHER	• Humid • Rain	• Cold • Strong sun
LIGHT LEVEL	• Low • Darkness	• Very bright
CLOTHES	• Too many	• Too few
EYES	• Closed	• Open wide
SLEEP	• Too much	• Too little
EXERCISE	• Too little	• Too much

Making Excuses

We all know how important regular exercise is for our well-being. And the best exercise regimes are those that are integrated into our lives. This holds true for meditation as well. Some of the many excuses people mention are summarized below, along with their remedies.

I don't have time. It is difficult to set aside twenty minutes each day to meditate. But, as already outlined, meditation actually makes time. However, you may have days when it is difficult to get the quiet time you need to settle down. To overcome this, I suggest practicing meditation on the train or bus, or taking ten minutes during a lunch break to sit in a park and watch your breath. Also, if finding a place for structured meditation is difficult, you can integrate some simple mindfulness meditations into your daily life. These are explained later in the chapter.

It's too noisy. When you first start meditation, it is important to practice in a quiet place. Like learning to ride a bike, when you start, you need an empty street in order to avoid bumping into anything. However, things will never be perfectly quiet. Even at home in your room, you may still hear a dog bark or a plane fly overhead. When you hear such noises, just be aware of the noise and return your focus to the object of meditation.

My body is too stiff for meditation. Some people say that they cannot meditate because they just can't sit still. Their bodies are not made for sitting in one place, and their joints are too stiff. To counter stiff joints, sit for only five minutes at a time (or as much as you can manage), and your body will thank you for being still.

Remember, most of this type of concern is your mind playing games with you.

I am too troubled. Some of the thoughts you observe may be disturbing. When you first start meditating, your mind is restless; it wants to keep thinking. Like anything in motion, the mind resists slowing down (Newton's second law of motion). Again, if you begin with a few minutes a day, you will find that you want to meditate more regularly. If you become aware of the thoughts occupying your heart and mind, you will start experiencing more peace, and eventually you will start looking forward to your meditation practice.

I have a headache. Ironically, pain is a great focusing tool for meditation. If you suffer from migraines you can use the pain as an object of meditation. Many meditators have experienced very favorable outcomes by meditating to treat their pain. Pain can focus the mind like no other meditation object.

A Journey and a Process, Not a Destination

Many of my students ask me, "What are we supposed to be feeling?" and "Am I on track?" These are hard questions to answer because the practice of meditation brings up so many different things for different people. There are some general progressions of experiences that many people report as they practice. Please take these as high-level guidelines rather than precise indications of what you should experience. The meditation experience differs for each of us, because it depends on one's individual state of mental resilience.

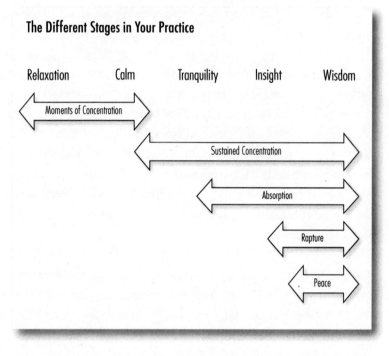

The Different Stages in Your Practice

Relaxation   Calm   Tranquility   Insight   Wisdom

Moments of Concentration

Sustained Concentration

Absorption

Rapture

Peace

Fleeting Moments of Concentration

Initially when you start meditating, you will need to concentrate on the meditation topic, which takes effort. You will get distracted and will consciously and continuously have to return your mind to the meditation focus, such as your breath. This can feel quite tiresome, because it takes energy to keep your mind in one place. You may feel that most of the meditation period is spent on things other than the meditation topic.

I have even heard of people getting headaches from trying too hard. If it's getting to this stage, shorten your meditation practice to a few minutes every day so that your ability to concentrate has time to develop.

Receiving the Gifts

As you journey along the path of meditation, you will experience milestones. These milestones are gifts you create for yourself.

Sustained Concentration

After a while you will experience sustained concentration. In this phase you will notice that you spend more time on the meditation object than drifting away from it. You may feel that you need to spend effort to keep your mind focused, but you no longer need to spend so much energy doing so.

Concentration can feel as if you're holding onto something so hard that you can see the whites of your knuckles. Sustained concentration lets you feel as if you are supporting something with open hands; it's a much more relaxed state.

Absorption

In the absorption stage you feel as if you are totally attuned to the meditation object. There is very little thinking outside the topic of meditation because you are so absorbed that you forget time and perhaps can't even hear what is going on around you. Imagine the feeling of being with someone you love; time seems to just fly, and you can't seem to spend enough time with your loved one. In this phase you can't wait to get back to your meditation session.

Rapture

Rapture happens when you are in awe of the meditation topic; you cannot think about anything else. If breath is your meditation topic, you feel as if each breath is your last and you just do not want to let go of it.

It may feel similar to experiencing a climax (of any sort) in which you are so engrossed and so full of the experience that you lose yourself. This resembles falling in love and staying up all night just so you can think about that person; it's hard to think about anything else.

When in rapture, you let go of all your concerns, plans, and fears; and you give yourself over entirely to the present moment. In this phase you may experience physical sensations such as goose bumps or your hair standing on end. Generally these are very pleasurable experiences.

Peace

At the peace stage of meditation, you have reached a state of equilibrium. You no longer feel any sense of lack in your life; you stop planning and worrying. You are just happy to be where you are at the present moment. It's a feeling of being satiated, full, complete, and at peace. You've reached your climax and are at peace, so there is no wanting or desiring.

You just want to be where you are. Because you are quiet and still, there is the space for your wisdom or creativity to start bubbling up. You feel lighter, because you can feel your disempowering thought patterns diminishing, and you start enjoying that experience of lightness and freedom.

Meditative Life — The Role of Mindfulness

Let's face it. It would be great to meditate every day, just as it would be great to exercise or eat five pieces of fruit every day. Unfortunately this may not happen. Even if you are not as disciplined as you might like to be all the time, you can still combine meditative aspects into your daily activities. It's something like knowing you should get to the gym for a full workout but, instead, walking rather than driving to where you need to go!

Known as mindfulness techniques, these methods allow you to incorporate meditation into ordinary activities throughout your day. Mindfulness differs from concentration in that it is more relaxed and supportive, whereas concentration can be perceived as tight and restrictive.

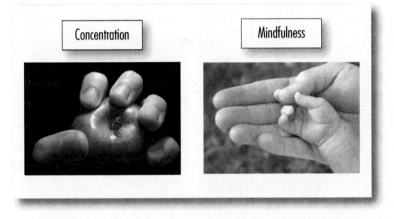

The key here is to have your mind so full of sensations that you experience solely from your senses, leaving no room for exhaustive mental chatter. This gives you the mental rest you need. It has very different effects on your mental state than concentration does, but it can prove to be a very powerful technique.

Awareness and attention allow you to live in the present moment. Normally the mind fluctuates between thoughts and feelings about the past, present, and future. Staying with your sensations allows you to be in the moment and helps train your mind to start letting go of detrimental thoughts.

All you have to do is what you are already doing, only with full attention. You need to avoid going on automatic pilot. Some describe the state of mindfulness as a beginner's mind. The best way to illustrate this is to imagine infants playing with a new toy. Rather than merely glancing at the toy, they really look at it, truly seeing everything in front of them. They sometimes bring it very close to their eyes. They might try to smell it and will squeeze it to feel the texture. They may try to hit it. But their full attention is focused on it. Children engage with objects from a sense of wonder that we adults unfortunately have forgotten.

To live in wonder is to have a wonder-full life.
ANONYMOUS

Of course, there are moments when we naturally have this mindfulness. For example, if we go on vacation to a new country, we are intensely interested in our surroundings. We take notice of the sounds, smells, and sights. Or when we make love to a new partner for the first time, we observe everything about that person with clarity, eager to savor every moment, every single sensation. I sometimes refer to mindfulness meditation as making love to the ordinary activities in our lives with extraordinary passion.

Mindfulness Training Exercises
Mindfulness Training Activity 1:
Eating Mindfully

Because eating is a very sensual activity, it is an easy and enjoyable way to have a meditative experience. The following activity is drawn from the website, www.mindfuleating.org and uses chips or fries. You can use any food (for example, pieces of fruit); the principle is the same.

Before eating the chips, become truly conscious of them. Smell the chips and enjoy their aroma. Feel them in your fingers.

Notice the salt and oil. Imagine yourself eating these chips in a meaningful way.

CHIP #1: Pick up one chip and look at it before you eat it. Notice its shape, colors, shadings, and curls. Now, eat this chip with total awareness. Take your time and be aware of each chew. Make eating this chip an experience in basic awareness.

CHIP #2: Take a second chip. You're going to notice the flavor of this chip as you eat it. Put it in your mouth, and chew it slowly and thoroughly. Pay attention to the tastes you experience. If you're eating a potato chip, notice the potato flavor; if it's some other kind of chip, notice that flavor. Keep chewing until it has been completely chewed up, and then swallow. Stop. Notice any aftertaste. Enjoy the chip to the maximum.

CHIP #3: With the next chip, you're going to notice textures. Pick up the third chip and look at it. Then put it in your mouth, but don't chew right away. Move your tongue against the chip, briefly exploring its edges, roughness, and so on. Now, begin chewing. Pay attention to how the textures change. Notice how your chewing creates new edges and new textures. Follow how these changes occur. Chew slowly and thoroughly and then swallow.

CHIP #4: Chewing creates noises, and with the next chip, you'll pay special attention to the sounds of eating. Put the fourth chip in your mouth and begin chewing. Listen carefully to every bite. Hear the sound of chewing and how it changes over time. Even when the chip has been thoroughly chewed, you can still hear some sounds from your mouth. Swallow after you've completely chewed the chip.[1]

By eating this way, you will have engaged all of your senses. When you intensely engage your senses, your mental chatter quiets down.

Mindfulness Training Activity 2: Showering Mindfully

Remember the last shampoo commercial you saw? Was the actor so engrossed in the act of shampooing her hair that she seemed overcome with joy?

When most of us take a shower, we are preoccupied with our plans for the day, such as what we intend to say and whom we plan to meet. However, showering can be an extremely sensuous experience if approached with mindfulness.

To practice mindfulness in the shower, try this. Before you start, anticipate the showering experience. Feel the texture of the metal faucet in your hands when you turn on the water. Notice the warmth of the water as it touches various parts of your body.

Listen to the water trickling down your body and then into the drain. Notice the sound of the water as it comes out of the showerhead.

Now hold the soap or shampoo. Notice the texture of the bar or bottle. Notice the smells and the feeling of soap on your skin. Listen to the sounds as you rub your body.

Notice the temperature of the water and your body. Notice how your mind wants to leave this fantastic sensual experience for something less sensual, such as solving a work problem or a relationship issue.

In the shower, try not to think about how wonderful the experience is; rather, try to merely switch on your senses to feel the various sensations on your body. Make a conscious effort to get out of your head and into your body.

Mindfulness Training Activity 3: Walking Mindfully

Walking meditation is easy to do and very effective. You can practice walking meditation in its own right, pacing very slowly up and down a predetermined path, or you can practice it between meetings or while shopping or walking to your car.

Again, this meditation is concerned with noticing what we feel and being aware of all the minute sensations. I tend to concentrate on sensing the feelings in my feet and the touch of air on my fingers as I walk.

Try this: if you need to walk to a meeting on a different floor or in another building, allow double the time you'd normally need so you can slow down on your way there. Start by noticing how you shift your weight off your chair. Notice the weight on your feet as you stand up.

Notice whether it feels light or heavy as you lift one leg to take your first step. Now notice how you engage your other leg to take the next step. As you walk, notice your rhythm and posture. Become aware of the feelings at the tips of your fingers as you move forward.

As you practice, you will notice more and more subtle yet exciting sensations. These will help you to drop your mental chatter and focus on being in the present moment. The subtler the sensation you focus on, the greater will be your level of absorption and mental rest. The list of mindfulness techniques is almost limitless. (For additional information, see Thich Nhat Hanh's book, *Peace Is Every Step: The Path of Mindfulness in Everyday*

Life.) Mindfulness techniques will certainly help you stay relaxed, calm, and tranquil.

Mindfulness Training Activity 4: Mindfulness at Traffic Lights

Have you ever noticed how many pedestrians ignore traffic lights? They seem to scoot across the road regardless of the signal, sometimes putting themselves in danger. Next time you are walking and come to a stoplight, just stop. Try to be physically and mentally still. Don't twitch or move; just fix your concentration on your breath and try to be absolutely present until the light turns green. You can do this in your car as well.

Continuing on the Mindfulness Journey

Remember, reading this book is only the beginning of your journey. If you are still reading, you probably have already started a very interesting journey, one that meditation will meander in and out of. There is much more to read and understand, and, even more important, much more to experience. Meditation is all about practice.

And, how will you gauge your progress? When life becomes a game that you play knowingly, you're on the journey. Once you believe this in your heart and mind, and experience it in your body, meditation will start to really work for you.

gratitude

I AM INDEBTED TO SO MANY for helping me write this book. If anything in this book helps you, it is from their hearts and minds.

Thank you to my darling Karishma, whose short, three-day life changed mine forever; my kids, Kavisha and Kailash, who allowed me to taste pure joy; Kiran, my bride of thirteen years, who taught me the essence of courage when she put her life on the line bringing our beautiful children into the world; Nanda, my teacher, who taught me the arts and philosophies of the ancient traditions; and my parents, Dr. Prakash and Kanika Sarma, who taught me their path and prepared me to create my own.

Thanks to all my friends and students for their suggestions and input into the creation of this book. And also thanks to Les Fallick for always being honest, no matter what; Elizabeth Broderick for always finding ways to be an absolutely exceptional friend; Behrad Behrady, my best pal, for his Muslim interpretation of the wonder of life; John Gibbons for his clinical psychologist's view of meditation; Dr. Sarjit Jassal for his Sikh insights; Dr. Jack Gray, not only for insights into Judaism, funds management, and pure mathematics but also, along with AMP Capital Investors, for showing deep levels of compassion and understanding during a particularly difficult period in my life; Bhante Tejadhammo for giving me an insight into the Buddhist path; Darren Bagshaw, my Mormon buddy, for being the warrior when I needed it the most; Dr. Paul Twomey for his friendship and Catholic view on life during all those long hours working together at McKinsey and beyond; Paul Fegan for his mentorship and support; Steven Gamerov for always believing that we can increase the level of consciousness in capitalism; Michael Rennie for being my friend at McKinsey and Company; Colin Pitt for his input on what makes great leaders; Stuart Beattie for his friendship, grammar style, and insights into Christian doctrines; and Ryan Glick and Adam Pozniack for being mensches.

Thanks to Rob Prugue, CEO of Lazard Asset Management Asia Pacific, for the infestation-of-fleas metaphor to illustrate the itchiness one gets when beginning meditation (see chapter 6).

Thanks to Shelly Kineisberg for editing and editing and editing and editing, and putting up with the *ands*. Thanks also to Jason Gardner, my editor at New World Library, and copy editor Nelda Street.

Thanks to the following people for providing me with inspiration and guidance: Brian Delaney, Dr. Ramesh Kumar, Mrs. Samyuktha Kumar, Sue Sharpe, Julie Storr, Janet Robertson, Emma Nicolls, Michael Kong, Michele Kahn, Joseph Scarcella, Nicola Atkinson, Rosamund Christie, Alison Low, Greg Low, Peter Rodowicz, Jane Bryson, Reg Bryson, David Corby, Jaspal Rekhraj, Tony Miracola, Joe Iaquinto, Mana Choudury, Lina Bose, Carina Hull, Stuart Lloyd-Hurwitz, Ian Bullock, Iain Goldman,

Manjit Singh, Catherine Hallinan, Rajeev Dewan, Peter Hope, Cairan McGuigan, and Shashi Kanagaratnam.

The stories I tell in this book have been told and retold for centuries. I have sourced them from many places. One great site is www.rider.edu/~suler/zenstory.

notes

Introduction

1. Maxwell Maltz, *Psycho-Cybernetics: A New Way to Get More Living Out of Life* (New York: Pocket Books, 1989).

Chapter 1: Meditation — Why Bother?

1. Bruce S. McEwen, "Protective and Damaging Effects of Stress Mediators," *The New England Journal of Medicine* 338 (January 15, 1998): 171–79, as quoted by Christopher Koch, "Managing Your Stress," *CIO* (August 1, 2003), www.cio.com/article /29578/Managing_Your_Stress.

2. Adapted from Eric Harrison, *Teach Yourself How to Meditate in Ten Simple Lessons: Discover Relaxation and Clarity of Mind in Just Minutes a Day* (Berkeley: Ulysses Press, 2001); Dharma Singh Khalsa and Cameron Stauth, *Meditation as Medicine: Activate the Power of Your Natural Healing Force* (New York: Atria, 2002).

3. Dharma Singh Khalsa and Cameron Stauth, *Meditation as Medicine: Activate the Power of Your Natural Healing Force* (New York: Atria, 2002).

4. B. K. Anand, G. S. Chhina, and B. Singh, "Some Aspects of EEG Studies in Yogis," *Electroencephalography and Clinical Neurophysiology* 13 (1961): 452–56.

5. A. Kasamatsu and T. Hirai, "An Electroencephalographic Study on the Zen Meditation (Zazen)," *Psychologia* 12 (1969): 205–25.

6. Sandra Blakeslee, "Study Suggests Meditation Can Help Train Attention," *New York Times*, May 8, 2007, psyphz.psych.wisc.edu /web/News/NYT_Med_0507.html; Lisa Takeuchi Cullen, "How to Get Smarter, One Breath at a Time," *Time Magazine*, January 10, 2006, www.time.com/time/magazine/article /0,9171,1147167,00.html.

7. Michael D. Lemonick, "The Biology of Joy," *Time Magazine*, January 9, 2005, http://www.time.com/time/magazine /article/0,9171,1015863,00.html.

8. Sara Lazar et al., "Meditation Experience Is Associated with Increased Cortical Thickness," *Neuroreport* 16 (17) (2005): 1893–97.

9. Jean L. Kristeller and C. Brendan Hallett, "An Exploratory Study of a Meditation-Based Intervention for Binge Eating Disorder," *Journal of Health Psychology* 4, no. 3 (1999): 357–63.

10. Jon Kabat-Zinn, "An Outpatient Program in Behavioral Medicine for Chronic Pain Patients Based on the Practice of Mindfulness Meditation: Theoretical Considerations and Preliminary Results," *General Hospital Psychiatry* 4 (1982): 33–47; Jon Kabat-Zinn, L. Lipworth, and R. Burney, "The Clinical Use of Mindfulness Meditation for the Self-Regulation of Chronic Pain," *Journal of Behavioral Medicine* 8 (1985): 163–90.

11. John Welwood, *Toward a Psychology of Awakening: Buddhism, Psychotherapy, and the Path of Personal and Spiritual Transformation* (Boston: Shambhala Publications, 2000), 143.

Chapter 2: Common Misconceptions about Meditation

1. John Welwood, *Toward a Psychology of Awakening: Buddhism, Psychotherapy, and the Path of Personal and Spiritual Transformation* (Boston: Shambhala Publications, 2000), 187.

2. Stephen R. Covey, *The Seven Habits of Highly Effective People* (New York: Free Press, 2004).

Chapter 4: A Model of the Mind

1. Allan W. Snyder, Elaine Mulcahy, Janet L. Taylor, D. John Mitchell, Perminder Sachdev, and Simon C. Gandevia, "Savant-like Skills Exposed in Normal People by Suppressing the Left Fronto-Temporal Lobe," *Journal of Integrative Neuroscience* 2, no. 2 (2003): 149–58, www.centreforthemind.com/images/savant skills.pdf.

2. Daniel Goleman, *Vital Lies, Simple Truths: The Psychology of Self-Deception* (New York: Simon and Schuster, 1996), 89.

3. J. Bendiner, *Biographical Dictionary of Medicine Facts on File* (New York: Facts on File, 1990); H. L. Bennett, D. R. Bensen, and D. A. Kuiken, "Preoperative Instruction for Decreased Bleeding during Spine Surgery," *Anesthesiology* 65 (1986): A245; H. L. Bennett and E. A. Disbrow, "Preparing for Surgery and Medical Procedures," in D. Goleman and J. Gurin, eds., *Mind-Body Medicine: How to Use Your Mind for Better Health* (Yonkers, NY: Consumer Reports Books, 1993), 401–27; H. L. Bennett and H. S. Davis, "Nonverbal Response to Intraoperative Conversation," *Anesthesia and Analgesia* 63(1984): 185; and H. L. Bennett, H. S. Davis, and J. A. Giannini, "Nonverbal Response to Intraoperative Conversation," *British Journal of Anaesthesia* 57 (1985): 174–79.

4. Rita Carter, *Mapping the Mind* (Berkeley: University of California Press, 2000); Howard Gardner, *Extraordinary Minds* (New York: Basic Books, 1998).

5. See note 1.

6. Anna Wise, *The High-Performance Mind: Mastering Brain Waves for Insight, Healing, and Creativity* (New York: Jeremy P. Tarcher, 1997).

7. Michael Gelb, *How to Think Like Leonardo da Vinci: Seven Steps to Genius Every Day* (New York: Dell Publishing, 1998).

Chapter 7: Developing a Relaxed State of Mind

1. Hans Seyle, *The Stress of Life* (New York: McGraw-Hill, 1978).
2. *The American Heritage Dictionary of the English Language*, fourth ed., s.v. "Relaxation," www.thefreedictionary.com/relaxation.
3. Brian Luke Seaward, *Managing Stress*, fifth ed. (Boston: Jones and Bartlett Publishers, 2005), 467.

Chapter 8: Becoming Deeply Calm

1. G. Keinan, "Decision Making under Stress: Scanning of Alternatives under Controllable and Uncontrollable Threats," *Journal of Personality and Social Psychology* 52, no. 3 (1987): 639–44.
2. William J. Elliott and Joseph L. Izzo, Jr., "Device-Guided Breathing to Lower Blood Pressure: Case Report and Clinical Overview," *Medscape General Medicine* 8, no. 3 (2006): 23.

Chapter 9: Developing Emotional Tranquility

1. "Monks in the Heat of Battle," as told by David Busch in *Culture-de-Sac*, university newsletter of Arizona State University Research, 1994, researchmag.asu.edu/stories/culturedesac.html.
2. Viktor E. Frankl, *Man's Search for Meaning* (London: Rider and Company, 2004), 66.
3. Dalai Lama and Victor Chan, *The Wisdom of Forgiveness: Intimate Conversations and Journeys* (New York: Riverhead Books, 2004), 48.
4. Steven Locke and Colligan Douglas, *The Healer Within: The New Medicine of Mind and Body* (New York: Plume Books, 1997), 242.
5. Thynn Thynn, *Living Meditation, Living Insight: The Path of Mindfulness in Daily Life* (Barre, MA: Center for Buddhist Studies, 2005), 30.

Chapter 10: Developing Insight

1. Bhante Henepola Gunaratana, *Mindfulness in Plain English* (Somerville, MA: Wisdom Publications, 1992), 3.
2. Candace B. Pert, *Molecules of Emotion: The Science Behind Mind-Body Medicine* (New York: Scribner, 1999).
3. Eugene T. Gendlin, *Focusing* (New York: Bantam Books, 1982).

Chapter 11: Cultivating Wisdom

1. A. Roger Merrill and Rebecca R. Merrill, *Life Matters: Creating a Dynamic Balance of Work, Family, Time, and Money*, abridged edition (New York: McGraw-Hill, 2003).
2. Ayya Khema, transcribed from a recording of her speech at Wat Buddha Dhamma Forest Monastery, Windsor, Australia (circa 1985).
3. Adapted from Jack Canfield and Victor Hansen, *Chicken Soup for the Soul*, 1st ed. (Deerfield Beach, FL: Health Communications, Inc., 1991), therein reprinted from "Another Way," with permission of The Putnam Publishing Group from Terry Dobson, *Safe and Alive: How to Protect Yourself, Your Family, and Your Property against Violence* (New York: Putnam, 1982).

Chapter 12: Bringing It All Together

1. This exercise is from the CAMP System, a website on mindful eating, www.mindfuleating.org/LivingCamp.html.

index

Page references given in *italics* refer to illustrations or material contained in their captions.

A

about the author

KAMAL SARMA HAD THE UNIQUE OPPORTUNITY of growing up with both Eastern and Western influences. He led the life of a typical Aussie kid until age thirteen, when he was sent away to finish school in an Indian ashram for five years. In this monastery environment, in addition to his training in meditation and yoga, he studied many world religions, including Christianity, Judaism, Islam, and Hinduism.

After leaving the ashram Kamal returned to Australia to pursue an international business career in management consulting, biotechnology, venture capital, and funds management. He has held senior positions in several organizations, including McKinsey and Company, Eli Lilly Pharmaceuticals, AMP Capital Investors, and St. George Bank.

Kamal's life was turned upside down after the death of his child. To overcome his grief and depression, he returned to his childhood training in mental resilience.

Currently Kamal is the director of Rezilium, a strategic leadership firm that works with senior executives to enhance their level of impact in the organizations they serve. He is also the cofounder of the Institute for Mental Resilience, which works to raise funds for orphanages around the world and provide solutions to inspire youth and counter youth suicide.

For over ten years Kamal has guided corporate executives in maintaining clarity and peace in their lives while meeting intense work demands and balancing their health and relationships. Please visit www.mentalresilience.com for more resources on mental resilience.